TRACING YOUR SHIPBUILDING ANCESTORS

A GUIDE FOR FAMILY HISTORIANS

Anthony Burton

Pen & Sword

FAMILY HISTORY

First published in Great Britain in 2010 by
PEN & SWORD FAMILY HISTORY
an imprint of
Pen & Sword Books Ltd
47 Church Street
Barnsley
South Yorkshire
S70 2AS

ISBN 978 1 84884 096 6

A CIP catalogue record for this book is
available from the British Library.

Typeset in Palatino and Optima by
Phoenix Typesetting, Auldgirth, Dumfriesshire

Printed and bound in England by
CPI UK

Pen & Sword Books Ltd incorporates the Imprints of
Pen & Sword Aviation, Pen & Sword Maritime, Pen & Sword Military,
Wharncliffe Local History, Pen & Sword Select, Pen & Sword Military
Classics and Leo Cooper.

For a complete list of Pen & Sword titles please contact
PEN & SWORD BOOKS LIMITED
47 Church Street, Barnsley, South Yorkshire, S70 2AS, England
E-mail: enquiries@pen-and-sword.co.uk
Website: www.pen-and-sword.co.uk

CONTENTS

PREFACE

Whenever one sits down to write any sort of history, there is always one question that has to be answered: which units do you use? A common problem in Britain comes with currency, where wages for example were, until the middle of the twentieth century, paid in pounds, shillings and pence. I have used the old monetary units, because that was what was actually paid. A workman in the early nineteenth century would get, say, 15s a week, not £0.75. So I have followed the convention of putting such sums in the old money first, with the modern equivalent in brackets afterwards. There remains the ever-present problem of making sense of money. Clearly, to take the example above, a wage of £0.75 would be ludicrous today, and we can only make sense of it by knowing what it would purchase two centuries ago. A convenient measure would be one of the basics of life: the loaf of bread. Our nineteenth-century man could buy 180 large loaves with his week's wage. So if, instead of thinking of his wage in terms of pounds, shillings and pence, we look at it in terms of loaves of bread, we can do a simple sum to get a modern equivalent. In order to buy a loaf today we would probably have to pay £1.50 so the 180-loaf wage is now equivalent to £270. It is always as well to remember that figures for costs, wages or anything else are only meaningful in terms of what the currency would buy at that time.

Units present rather more of a problem when it comes to physical measurements. We have gone metric but our forebears used the old Imperial measures and a straight conversion often leads to seemingly illogical results. Why, for example, would an engineer build a steam engine with a 45.72cm diameter cylinder? The answer, of course, is that he did nothing of the kind. He built, as accurately as he possibly could, one with an 18-in cylinder. Although using metrical measures instead of feet and inches does not always produce quite the same sort of absurdities, I have preserved the original units. They are the ones the designer worked in. There is one unit, at least, that has remained unchanged for centuries – the knot. This is a speed of 1 nautical mile per hour, the nautical mile being 6,080ft compared with 5,280ft for the miles we measure on the road. Why this difference? The answer is that the nautical mile is far more useful to the navigator at sea, working with charts. It is basically equivalent to one minute of latitude, so anyone with a chart can measure off distances using a pair of dividers, regardless of the scale of the map. This means that a speed of 30 knots, for example, is roughly equivalent to 34.5 miles per hour.

The name 'knot' takes us right back to the age of sailing ships. In order to measure speed a specially shaped piece of heavy wood, the 'log', was attached to a rope and thrown overboard. The rope had knots at set intervals. As the ship sailed away, the log remained floating where it was left, and as the rope was gradually paid out, the number of knots that passed through the sailor's hand was counted for a set period of time. The result was entered in the log book. It is difficult to believe that when I log in on my computer I am making a connection with someone throwing a piece of wood off a sailing ship. It is interesting to note how many terms from the world of seafaring have entered everyday use, emphasising the fact that Britain is a maritime nation. So it should not be too surprising to find that most of us, at some time or other, had connections with ships and the sea. I hope this book will help the reader make one of those connections – with those who built the ships that once crossed the oceans of the world.

PICTURE CREDITS

Illustrations on pages x, 9, 13, 35, 36, 38, 41, 45, 46, 59, 67, 69, 78, 115, Anthony Burton; 15, 17, The Master and Fellows, Magdalene College, Cambridge; 23, British Library; 25, 70, Gwynedd Archives; 26, Whitehaven Museum; 64, Scottish Maritime Museum; 68, 80, Glasgow Museums, The People's Palace; 75, Yarrow Shipbuilders Ltd; 82, Clyde Shipping Co.; 83, Tyne and Wear Archives; 87, 103, Strathclyde Regional Archives; 93, Working Class Movement Library; 98, Business Records Centre, University of Glasgow; 105, Scottish Record Office; 117, North News and Pictures.

INTRODUCTION

There has probably never been an industry anywhere that offered its workforce a prouder moment than the day on which a great ship was launched, sliding down the slipway to leave the land behind and take its rightful place out on the water. On that day every single person who worked on the vessel would turn out to watch and would bring their families along to share the occasion. The fact that this is an industry with such a romantic end product adds an extra level to the interest and pleasure of researching family history. There is the possibility, in imagination at least, that we can travel back in time and share in the pride and excitement of that great day. Which is why, having once discovered a connection to the industry, we want to know more. What did that particular yard make? What sort of ships did my ancestor work on? Is there any chance that I might be able to identify a particular vessel? It will not often be possible to be that specific, but let me give an example from my own family history as a form of encouragement.

My great-grandfather was one of three brothers who set up a business manufacturing marine boilers at Stockton-on-Tees in 1869. I knew very little about the firm, but slowly, with the help of relatives and the local history museum, I began to acquire information and eventually found photographs of the actual boilers and details in trade advertisements. I did not expect to get any further than that, but I did discover that a large part of the business consisted of providing boilers for steam drifters for the herring fleets of East Anglia. There is one lone survivor from the hundreds of vessels, *Lydia Eva*, now preserved at Lowestoft and awaiting restoration. And, yes, she is indeed fitted with a Riley Brothers boiler. In the town of Stockton, all that remains of the works is a street name, Riley Street, but at least one boiler has survived, not just in any old vessel, but in the very last steam drifter. It is this sort of discovery that makes researching family history in this industry so especially rewarding.

In the case of my family, the connection with the industry was at once clear and obvious. This is not always the case, but in a maritime nation there is always the possibility that shipbuilding will appear somewhere in the family line. My wife's family was from Cornwall. Her great-grandfather, Thomas Rogers, was born near Bodmin and the first reference to his working life is as a farm labourer. He moved on from there to train as a

A ship's boiler leaving the Riley Brothers works at Stockton-on-Tees.

blacksmith. By 1862 he had moved to Stoke Damarel, a name that has all but disappeared off the modern map of Britain. What sort of place was this? If you look at the freeholder lists for the eighteenth century then you find no fewer than fifteen shipwrights listed, as well as associated trades, such as rope makers and sail makers. Why has such a seemingly important place vanished? The answer is simple: it has been swallowed up in the expansion of Devonport, and that is where Thomas Rogers, the blacksmith, had gone to work, in the naval dockyard. There are important points to make here. First, it is not just the more obvious trades that indicate a job in shipbuilding. There are others in the Stoke Damarel freeholder rolls who might just as easily have been working at the dockyard. The carpenters and joiners, for example, might have been building barns and making furniture, or they could have been fitting out cabins on warships. There is no way of knowing without further research. Shipbuilding required a lot of men, some skilled and some unskilled, and what they did and how they worked will be dealt with later in the book. The other fact that emerges is that social mobility is no new phenomenon. Thomas Rogers, who had started out as a farm worker, stayed only briefly at Devonport, before moving on again to work on armaments at the Woolwich Arsenal. The fact that there is no strong family tradition of

working in shipbuilding does not mean that there is no connection somewhere down the line.

This brief glimpse of two specific family histories shows just how diverse
the shipbuilding industry is, with one side of the family working in a naval
dockyard in south-west England and the other making boilers for fishing
vessels in the north-east. Before developing this theme, this is a good point
at which to pause and try and define what we actually mean by shipbuilding. The answer is not as obvious as it might seem. The first thing you
have to decide is what you mean by a ship. This was once a very precise
term, referring to sea-going vessels with three or more masts and square-
rigged, which is not particularly helpful. For the purposes of this book, the
essential lies in the first part of the definition – sea-going. We shall not be
looking at the many small yards, making boats for use on rivers and canals.
Even that does not quite solve the problem. Do you, for example, include
the forge workers who manufactured the iron or steel plates for a ship's
hull? The great liners of the past could never have been built without them.
But these were companies supplying raw material for many other projects
as well, so I have not included them, though they will get mentioned from
time to time. Basically, we are looking at people who worked in yards
from which large sea-going vessels were launched and fitted out.
Geographically, these are spread all round the coast and for some distance
up major rivers. We tend to think of shipyards as having been concentrated
on just a few major centres, but this has not always been the case.

Right up to the middle of the nineteenth century, most activity was
concentrated in southern England. All that changed when wooden ships
powered by sails began to give way to iron vessels driven by steam. The
age of wooden ships needed yards close to reliable sources of timber: those
building steamers needed to be near foundries and forges. The transformation also meant that ships were getting bigger and bigger, and that in
turn meant the vessels needed to be launched into deep water on broad
rivers. While shipbuilding grew on the banks of Clyde or Tyne, it declined
on the Thames and Avon. But all the time the industry as a whole was
expanding. It has been estimated that in the early years of the nineteenth
century, there were perhaps 20,000 men working in the industry. At the
peak of production that number had risen to over 300,000. This was a
period, in the years leading up to the First World War, when British shipbuilders dominated world markets, producing more than four times the
tonnage of each of their nearest rivals, Germany and the USA. Britannia
really did rule the waves.

In the years after the First World War, depression set in, not just in Britain,
but around the world. British yards, however, were particularly badly hit.
The home fleet scarcely grew, and the overseas market was the worst

affected, as other countries began developing and modernising their own industries. There was a brief respite during the Second World War, when the yards were all working, building warships and replacements for the merchant fleet, as more and more ships were lost in action. But it was no more than a respite, and the decline has continued right up to the present day. The great days and the world our forebears knew have gone for ever, which adds poignancy to the study of British shipbuilding and the people who worked in the industry. In the following chapters we shall be looking at both the enterprise that made Britain a nation of shipbuilders to the world, and the problems that caused it to lose that place to foreign competitors.

The study of family history is now extremely well documented and although there will be advice on how to get started, the main emphasis will be on helping researchers to find and use the sources that are unique to this particular industry.

TRACING YOUR SHIPBUILDING ANCESTORS

Chapter One

GETTING STARTED

*Starting research – Published sources and museums –
Basic family history documents – Shipbuilding archives*

Starting research

The starting point for researching family history is the same, whatever the occupation that is being investigated: talk to the family. Try and speak to as many members as you possibly can, not just parents and grandparents, but include uncles, aunts and even the most distant cousins. You never know who might have the crucial document or vital snippet of information that will help to fill gaps in the history. Anecdotes and stories can give valuable clues to the past, but you need to treat such information with caution. Memories are notoriously unreliable: almost anyone doing this kind of research will be told, for example, that a member of the family was born in such and such a town, only to find when documentary evidence becomes available that they were actually born miles away, even in a different county. There is also the real possibility now that genealogy has become so popular that one member of the family will have already started on a similar task and will have consequently acquired a lot of information that can be shared. Here again one has to exercise certain caution: a distant relation of mine produced a family tree according to which I had married my own mother!

   A very useful way of checking if anyone has already started on a similar process is to join a family history society. These are generally based on counties, and many societies publish lists of members' interests. Shipbuilding is a localised industry and it is quite common to find generations of workers employed at the same yards, so this focus on a particular region can prove very fruitful. It is a huge advantage to be able to build on research done by others, and it is not by any means a one-way system. As you begin to get deeper into the subject you might well find that you in turn can help in supplying information to those following different branches of the family. For example, I recently looked at the correspondence relating to a particular family with shipbuilding connections in Sunderland, and it was fascinating to see how one simple question resulted in a flood of information.

Published sources and museums

Once you have established a connection with shipbuilding, you will certainly want to know more about the industry and the people who worked in it. It is probably best to start with a basic general introduction, such as this, and then perhaps move on to a more-detailed general history and local histories. Although there are large numbers of books on ships and the sea, there are very few that offer an overall view of the shipyards that made them. I am suggesting my own book not through vanity, but simply because I have been unable to find any other general history published in recent years. There are, however, published histories of many individual yards, not merely the big and famous, which can prove fascinating. The great majority of them are out of print, though you should be able to get copies through your local library. Failing that you might have to go to specialist libraries, such as that at the National Maritime Museum. The copyright libraries hold copies of most books published in Britain. The British Library is the best known, but you may find it more convenient to use the National Libraries of Wales or Scotland, or the Library of Trinity College, Dublin. Once you find a connection with a particular yard, you may want to try and find a copy to buy for yourself. Many of the books are beautifully produced, with excellent illustrations. Nowadays most second-hand bookshops have Internet connections and can help track down a specific volume. Alternatively you can do the job yourself on the computer by logging on to www.AbeBooks.co.uk or www.bookfinder.com, two sites that will give you access to thousands of dealers.

Reading about a subject will help you to come to terms with the history of the industry and what it did, but it is equally valuable to be able to see an actual yard to get an understanding of how it worked and see the artefacts that were used. The general public are not generally admitted to working yards, but there are a number of museums based on former shipyards. They range from the immense site of the Historic Dockyard at Chatham to the shipbuilding village of Buckler's Hard in Hampshire. Some of these may have special facilities for dealing with family history queries, but even if they do not the curatorial staff may often be able to help with specific queries. Many of the maritime museums spread around the country also have excellent sections dealing with shipbuilding. Equally important are the many historic ships preserved around the coast and there are a number of replicas of famous ships, built using old technology. It really does help in bringing the whole subject to life, when you can actually study a vessel in this way. For example, seeing the interior of the hull of a wooden ship makes one realise how intricate ship construction is, and how much skill is required to create the optimum shape. A ship does not even have to be fully restored to make it interesting, in fact it is often easier to see construction details at an early stage of restoration than it is when the ship is looking as grand and as fresh as when she was launched. For example, I was fortunate enough to visit Britain's first ironclad battleship HMS *Warrior* before restoration work was started and I found it at least as interesting as when I went to see her after completion. In her rough condition, when little had survived apart from the basic hull and decks, it was very much simpler to understand how the unique system of armour plating had been put together.

Published books and museum visits will only take you part of the way in your researches. Many, many yards have closed without their histories being written up. The site will have been cleared and artefacts sold or dumped. Fortunately many archives have been preserved and these will form an essential part of your research. By far the best starting point is the guide to historical records edited by L A Ritchie, *The Shipbuilding Industry* (1992). It gives details on documents relating to some 200 privately owned British yards, trade organisations and public records concerning the industry. Most of the latter can be found at the National Archives. In practice, the majority of the papers are held in a few major archives. The main archives for the north east are the Tyne and Wear Archives held in Newcastle upon Tyne. The main sources for the Clyde are the Business Records Centre at the University of Glasgow, the Mitchell Library, Glasgow and the Glasgow Museum of Transport. Mersey shipyard records are held at the Birkenhead Reference Library and the Merseyside Maritime Museum. The records for Northern Ireland are mostly held in the Public Record Office of Northern Ireland in Belfast. The majority of the papers relating to naval dockyards are either in the Public Record Office at Kew or in the National Maritime Museum at Greenwich. Between them these bodies hold a very high proportion of available records, but by no means all. They cover most of the major employers, but one must never forget the immense number of smaller yards scattered all around the country, whose records have to be hunted down in local archives and museums.

Nowadays the first stop for most researchers is not the sometimes far distant library or museum but the computer. More and more information is being made available online. Even if you don't have your own computer, most libraries of any size now make them available at a very small cost per session. Even complete novices soon find how easy it is to use the Internet, but as with all research there is a danger. The material available online is only as reliable as the person who put it there, and there are all too many sites offering either very dubious facts or information that is downright wrong. It is safest to regard the Internet as a guide to reliable, checkable sources, rather than the final stopping place. Obviously, this depends to a large extent on the nature of the site. Where a site is run by a government agency or some other officially recognised body then one can be reasonably confident of its accuracy.

The Internet is also a very good starting point for those who are just coming to grips with family history. Most people by now are familiar with search engines, such as Google, but simply tapping in 'Shipbuilding' for example will start you off with a page showing the first 10 of over 5 million entries. There is such a vast amount of information available that it is easy to get over-whelmed by it all. So a complete novice, or even someone who is familiar with the Internet but not with looking for family history sites, might well want to start with a guide aimed specifically at family history researchers. There are two books of particularly use: Peter Christian's *The Genealogist's Internet* (2005), produced by the National Archive, and Stuart A Raymond's *Family History on the Web* (2004), for the Federation of Family History Societies.

Once you are comfortable with using the Internet, you will find there are a number of key sites that will help direct you to the specific information you require. The National Register of Archives is invaluable. It does not hold any actual documents, but it does tell you where they are to be found in England and Wales. Altogether it holds 44,000 lists and catalogues. Obviously you are not going to want to search the whole lot, but the website leads you through various steps that will narrow down the search. Turning to www.nationalarchives.gov.uk/nra will give you an overall view of how the site works, and the different categories that can be consulted. It lists businesses, organisations, personal papers, family documents and diaries, all of which can be accessed individually. For example, under organisations you can call up a full list of trade unions, arranged alphabetically. You can then quickly locate documents relating to individual unions, such as the Amalgamated Union of Shipbuilding, Engineering and Constructional Workers, and discover that the Union records for 1921 are held at Warwick University. On the more general subject of shipbuilding as a whole, the starting point depends on how much information you have. But even if all you know is that you have a relative who worked in shipbuilding in a certain area at a certain rough date that should be enough to begin. Turn to www.nationalarchives.gov.uk/a2a. This opens the A2A site, where you can make a start by entering a keyword in the box. Simply typing 'shipbuilding' turns up nearly 2,000 entries, but this can be narrowed down very quickly, by entering information on the region and the dates in which you are interested. For example, asking for details for Newcastle between 1900 and 1950 reduces the number of entries to a manageable fourteen. This is a very useful website to turn to at any stage in your research, and is particularly valuable once you have at least a rough idea of the places and periods in which you are particularly interested.

One approach might seem so obvious that it is easily overlooked. It is always worth simply putting a name into the search engine to see what comes up. Needless to say, it helps if your family name isn't Smith or Jones. The point is, it only takes a moment to do and you just might turn out lucky. For most of us, however, there is only one option, and that is to proceed through a series of logical steps.

Basic family history documents

Having talked to members of the family, the first essential is to record your findings as soon as possible, and to continue keeping the records as you work your way through the family tree. The next step is to acquire firm documentary evidence in the form of birth, marriage and death certificates. These are held at the Government Record Office (GRO) and records from 1900 onwards can be accessed and ordered on line. The starting point is www.familyrecords.gov.uk. Births, marriages and deaths have been recorded for England and Wales since 1837. Records for Scotland began in 1855 and are available from the GRO for Scotland and the appropriate website for starting the search is www.gro-scotland.gov.uk. Records for Northern Ireland started in 1864 and details are at www.groni.gov.uk, though only Protestant marriages are recorded. This is not as big a problem as it might seem, since for much of its history the major employer in Ireland, Harland and Wolff, employed a predominantly Protestant work-force, and for a time banned Catholics altogether. There are a few snags of which you should be aware. Records are listed under the office where the details were registered. It is perfectly possible that a baby might have been born in a hospital in one town but for the birth to be registered some time later in another town where the parents lived.

The birth certificate can provide a wealth of information. It will give the mother's maiden name, assuming she was married, which will help in taking the story back another generation on her side of the family. Up to

1875, a mother could have the father's name included, whether she was married or not, and did not even require the father's permission. After that date, the father could refuse and the section could be left blank. In some cases, the father's occupation could also be included. Marriage certificates carry additional useful information, including the ages of bride and groom. These are generally reliable, but not always. A young couple marrying without their parents' consent, for example, could easily add a few years to their age to get round the problem. Assuming the age is accurate, it is an obvious help in working back towards the birth certificates. The certificate will also give details of occupations and parentage. Death certificates often seem to be less valuable as sources of information, but they can be helpful in searching for wills and burial places. They also provide information on occupation, but not always in the case of women. A classic example of the lack of importance attached to women's work is the case of Florence Nightingale. The most famous nurse in the world has her occupation given as 'Daughter of William Nightingale'. This latter point is not so important in the case of shipbuilding as, apart from during war years, very few women were ever employed. One entry that can prove interesting is the cause of death: this was an industry with a high rate of fatal accidents.

The next vital source of information is the census. The first census in Britain was held in 1801, extended to Ireland in 1821 and has been held every decade since then, with the exception of 1941. The results are generally subject to a hundred-year rule to protect privacy, but the 1911 returns are now available for England, Wales and Ireland, but not for Scotland at the time of writing. They can all be accessed at the different National Archives, where they can be consulted free of charge. They are also available online from www.nationlarchives.gov.uk/census for England and Wales, www.scotlandspeople.gov.uk for Scotland and www.national-archives.ie for Irish returns for 1901 and 1911, most earlier records having been destroyed.

The earliest returns for the first four censuses, 1801–31, were simply head counts and are of little practical value for family historians, so to all intents and purposes these documents will only lead back as far as 1841. From that time on, the census questionnaire was extended to give ever more information. As with all the documents discussed so far, there are benefits and problems. The census return listed all the people staying at a particular address on the specified day with their full names, ages, occupations, relationships to the head of household and place of birth. Some problems arise because so many people were illiterate in the nineteenth century, and had to have forms filled in by someone else. Names might be misspelled and information misunderstood and, of course, the people listed had no means of checking what was recorded. These are, however, comparatively minor problems, given the value of the information that a census entry contains. Not only does the census entry provide facts for that year, but it also provides a useful starting point for delving back even further in time. An obvious item of interest is the section on employment, but to make full use of it you will need to know the name of the various jobs in the shipbuilding industry, a subject that will be dealt with more fully later in the book.

If you succeed in taking your history back to the middle of the nineteenth century then you will have to turn to other sources to continue the search. Now you will have to look for parish records. Baptisms and marriages were registered from 1538 onwards and the documents were originally held in the local churches. Very few are there today, most having been transferred to county record offices or local studies libraries. As one would expect, given the time span, these records are far from complete, but a surprisingly large number have survived. Even some of those that are missing from the parish collections can turn up elsewhere. From 1598 all parish priests had to send a copy of their registers to the bishop. Known as the Bishops' Transcripts, these can often fill in gaps in the local records. One organisation, the Church of Jesus Christ of Latter-day Saints, has carried out a research programme into these documents and has made the results widely available through the International Genealogical Index which currently has some 800 million entries, recording births, baptisms and marriages. This can be accessed online at www.familysearch.org for British entries. Local branches of the church may also be able to help and a number of libraries hold copies.

The final class of document of general interest is the will. This can prove an absolutely fascinating document, providing a snapshot of a person's life. The most obvious information it gives is an indication of just how wealthy the individual was – and in general it was only the comparatively well off who bothered to make wills at all. There may also be specific items that are listed to be passed on, though few will be as thought-provoking as Shakespeare's famous 'second best bed'. My own great-grandfather's will, for example, showed that although he had invested mainly in the family business, he had also taken shares in other ventures in the shipping industry. He left shares in a variety of shipbuilding companies, including a substantial holding in the local Ropner Shipbuilding & Repair Co. of his home town Stockton. This was particularly appropriate as his house backed onto the public park given to the town by Ropner. It obviously made good sense to keep on good terms with the most important local customer. He also put money into the final product, investing small amounts in a number of steamship companies. For me, this provides an insight into the complexities of an industry in which companies that provided components of ships, such as boilers, had to keep a close eye on all aspects of the shipping world. Ordinary shipyard workers would not have had such elaborate wills, but they can provide a different sort of insight. It is often the case that a specialist craftsman would pass on his tools to a later generation, for example, and these could well be the most valuable part of the legacy.

During the period 1384 to 1858 wills were proved by ecclesiastical courts, of which the most important was the Prerogative Court of Canterbury and the records are held in the National Archive. They are mainly for comparatively wealthy citizens, living in southern England and Wales. Details can be found on the website listed above, and there is also an index that enables you to search by occupation as well as name. There is a small fee for downloading the documents from www.nationalarchives.gov.uk/documentsonline. Although the vast majority of workers in the industry scarcely qualified as being well off, shipwrights at the royal dockyards are well represented among the thousands of entries.

The system changed in 1858, after which wills went either to the local probate registries or the main office in London. Many of these wills can be accessed at local archives and libraries as well as the National Archive. Copies are available for a fee from the Probate Registry office in York. Scottish wills from 1500 to 1901 can be seen online at www.scotlandspeople.gov.uk. Most of the wills held in the Irish National Archive were destroyed in a fire of 1922. The earlier records from 1484 to 1858 are listed in a special index that can be browsed at www.irishorigins.com.

Shipbuilding archives

Printed documents are not the only items of interest to the family historian, and this is especially true when it comes to shipbuilding. Photographs of shipbuilding date right back to the very beginning of photography. William Fox Talbot, the pioneer of photography, took a picture of the SS *Great Britain* as she was being fitted out in 1844. This is believed not only to be the first ever photograph of shipbuilding, but also the very first taken of any ship. Many of the archives listed in this book have excellent photographic collections. But photographs are by no means the only form of illustration available. Just before Fox Talbot took his picture, artists were on hand to record the launch of the great iron ship. And although shipyards were generally considered rather less romantic subjects than the vessels themselves there are many illustrations of shipbuilding activities, some dating right back to medieval times. Equally fascinating are the plans and drawings produced by the shipwrights. Many people have difficulty 'reading' naval architects' drawings, and that included many of the ship

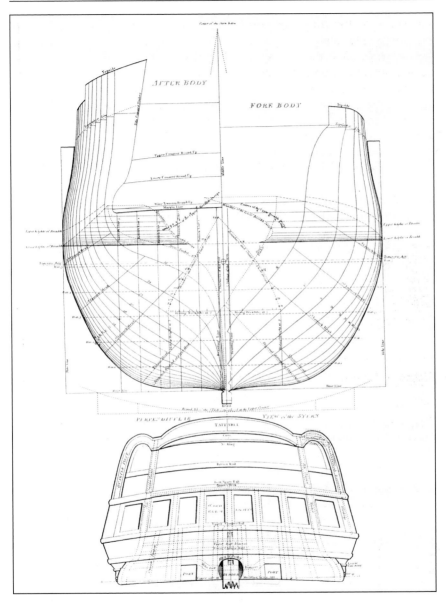

A naval architect's drawing of c. 1800 showing the shape of the hull at various points along the length: not easy to interpret by anyone but the expert.

owners who were ordering the vessels. So the yards commissioned models to show exactly what the owners would get for their money. People often think that the ship models in museums were like other models, made as copies of the real thing – but in shipbuilding they were generally made before actual work on the vessel had even begun. Some were full models, showing every aspect of the ship in great detail: others were half-models, designed specifically to show the shape of the hull. There are outstanding collections, particularly those of the main maritime museums, and museums in major shipbuilding centres, such as Newcastle and Glasgow.

The aim of this chapter has been to concentrate on the basics of family history research, with only a few passing glances at shipbuilding. Now we can start to look at the history of the industry itself and start to follow some rather more specialised lines of enquiry.

Chapter Two

THE WOODEN SHIP

Early ships

No one really knows when the first vessel left the shores of Britain and headed out into the deep, turbulent waters of the open sea. Looking back into the distant past the best we have are the fragile remains of ancient vessels, covering centuries of history, with immense gaps in our knowledge that will probably never be filled. What we can say with certainty is that wooden ships, capable of putting to sea, were being built in the Bronze Age over 4,000 years ago. We know that because the remains of three of these craft were found buried in the mud of the Humber estuary at North Ferriby. One of them was successfully lifted and was sufficiently well preserved for a detailed examination to be possible. There was a 43.5ft (13.2m) long keel constructed from two oak planks and curving upwards at bow and stern. These were joined together at the centre of the keel by an overlapping joint, known as a 'scarf' or 'scarph' – a technique that was to continue in use for as long as wooden keels were built. The keel formed the base from which the sides of the hull were then built up using thinner planks. That is about all we know about this prehistoric craft, and the next archaeological find takes us forward in time by a massive leap of some 2,000 years.

Excavations of a Saxon burial site at Sutton Hoo, Suffolk revealed a remarkable discovery. Here in the seventh century AD a king was buried in a great ship, surrounded by his richest possessions. The treasures survived, but the timbers of the ship itself rotted away leaving no more than a shadowy imprint in the sand. But even the traces were very revealing. This was a graceful vessel roughly 90ft (27m) long, 14ft (4m) beam, with a maximum depth of slightly over 3ft (1m). She was rowed by forty oars, and although it is possible a sail was used, the traces have all vanished. Steering was by means of a board hung over the right side of the ship looking towards the bows – hence the name 'steerboard' later simplified to the familiar 'starboard'. It would have been difficult to moor with that side of the vessel against the harbour wall, because the steering board could have been damaged. So vessels were tied up with the opposite side next to the quay – the port side.

The construction is much more sophisticated than in the North Ferriby vessels. The keel ends in separate stem and stern posts, and the sides were built up by overlapping planks held together by metal rivets. The hull was strengthened with twenty-six internal wooden frames. This method of construction, known as clinker building, would be familiar to anyone building a wooden boat even today and was the basis for ship construction right up to the sixteenth century. There was a limit to what could be learned from Sutton Hoo, but another vessel, discovered at Graveney in Kent, literally provided more solid evidence. This craft was constructed shortly before the Norman Conquest and the main timber used in construction was English oak – the old song 'Heart of oak are our ships' has a literal meaning. The planks were joined to the frame by means of wooden pegs, known as treenails. To keep the hull watertight the spaces between the planks were stuffed with twisted hair. This technique, known as caulking, has remained an essential part of wooden shipbuilding ever since. The caulking material, which in later years was mainly oakum made from strands of old rope, was driven into place by means of a caulking iron. This looks like a wide-bladed chisel that is hammered by a mallet to push the material deep into the gaps. The final touch was to cover the seams with tar.

The remarkable thing about the Graveney ship is that any shipwright looking at it at any time in the succeeding centuries would have known exactly what had been done and how. The essentials of the technology scarcely changed over the years. The big evolutionary steps were not in hull construction but in the way in which ships were moved, the development of sails.

The early ships of northern Europe carried a single square sail on one mast. The Viking long ship is the obvious example. Later the sail area was extended by adding a second sail above the main, a topsail. This is a rig that has survived in the Humber keel, one of the many different kinds of vessels that carried cargo on Britain's rivers and on short coastal voyages up until

The Humber keel Comrade *shows many of the characteristics of the medieval ship.*

quite recently. Over the centuries, more masts and more sails were added as ships got bigger and bigger. Further south in the Mediterranean a different tradition developed, based on triangular or lateen sails. These can still be seen in dhows that trade across the Arabian Sea and the feluccas of the Nile. Unlike the square sail, the lateen can be turned round the mast to take the wind on either side, making for greater mobility and enabling the vessel to sail close to the wind. As with the square sails, vessels were developed carrying lateen sails on more than one mast, culminating in the three-masted vessels known as caravels. Eventually the two technologies were married in the carracks. These combined the driving power of the square sail with the manoeuvrability of the lateen. Carracks and caravels were the vessels that took European explorers across the Atlantic to discover the New World.

Early naval vessels were basically floating platforms for the fighting men. Archers, for example, shot at the enemy from castles in bow and stern. These superstructures were later adapted for more peaceful use – the forecastle became the fo'c'sle, where the crew lived, and the aft castle the poop deck.

The other major constructional changes could be seen in the hull. Gradually clinker building was abandoned for larger ships in favour of carvel building. Here the ship was constructed by setting out regular frames, rising up from the keel and attaching planks to the outside so that they abutted instead of overlapping. This gave a smooth outer skin that offered less resistance to the water than the uneven surface of the clinker-built ship. The hull was strengthened by means of horizontal beams attached to right-angled wooden brackets, known as 'knees'. The knees had to support both the beams and the decking, so they needed to be strong and had to be made out of a single piece of wood, in which the grain ran true. The oak was favoured, because the branches tend to grow at right angles to the trunk. It was possible to cut a knee at the joint to make what was known as 'compass timber'. It also became common practice to plank the inside of the hull. A further big improvement came with the abandonment of the steer board in favour of the rudder, hung off the stern post. Originally this could only be moved by means of a massive tiller, eventually replaced by the steering wheel. The ship had become a complex machine. To move the sails and spars required a complex system of ropes and pulleys, known as blocks, which formed the running rigging. More lines and blocks were needed to stabilise the masts – the standing rigging.

Shipyard workers

A whole range of trades were now involved in shipbuilding. There were the master shipwrights who were responsible for the overall design and construction of the vessel. The workforce of craftsmen and labourers was under their direct control. The work itself was a mixture of specialist skills and hard labour. The basic tasks entailed cutting and shaping the timber, and assembling it on site to create the hull. The first job generally consisted of sawing the matured timber, and this was done in the saw pit. The log was laid over the pit, and was cut using a two-man saw. One man stood at the top of the pit, and he pulled the saw up: his colleague stood at the

An illustration from Matthew Baker, Fragments of Ancient Shipbuilding, *showing a shipyard worker of the 1580s carrying a wooden knee.*

bottom of the pit and he was responsible for the down stroke. In theory, the top sawyer had the harder task, but the man at the bottom had the more uncomfortable job, constantly working in a cloud of sawdust. The simplest shape was the rectangular plank, but ship construction is not like building a house, where everything can be built in straight lines. Some of the planks have to be bent to fit the curves of the hull, and these could be solid timbers, many inches thick, not lengths of plywood. First the planks had to be heated in a steam chest to make them pliable. The chest itself consisted of a box, big enough to hold a whole plank, with a boiler at one end. After steaming the plank would have softened and it was then all a matter of working quickly and accurately to fit it to the frame before it hardened again. It was a tough and demanding job, manhandling heavy pieces of timber and exerting constant pressure to hold them in place until they were securely fixed.

This part of the work was largely manual labour. The far more skilled work came when it was necessary to produce curved timbers for elements such as ribs and knees. The big timbers for the main frame of the hull had to be shaped using a very specific tool, the adze. This is not unlike an axe, except that the blade is at right angles to the shaft, not aligned with it. In use, the adze was not raised and brought down like an axe, but swung rather like a croquet mallet. When brought down into the timber, it naturally moved through the arc of a circle, so that each cut was curved. The use of the adze required a great deal of skill, if the final shaped piece was to be smooth and regular. Visit any old ship and if you look at the timbers of the frame, you will still see the marks left by the adze.

Other woodwork was more like that of any carpenter, involving drilling, chiselling, planing and so forth, but some work required a very high degree of artistry. Older ships often had decorative features, of which the carved figurehead is the best known. Even more elaborate decoration could be seen at the stern, an elaborate system of scrolls and carvings known as 'gingerbread', which was often gilded to increase the ornamental effect. The appearance would be far less striking without the gold paint – you would be literally taking the gilt off the gingerbread. The carpenters entrusted with this work were among the most highly regarded in the shipyard.

One of the most important tasks in fitting out the ships went to the riggers. It was their responsibility to assemble the whole complex system of blocks and ropes to ensure that the ship was stable and could be worked efficiently. The first to be set in place were the shrouds, which run from the masthead to both port and starboard, where they were fastened to the ship's sides at the chain-plates. The shrouds were held together by horizontal ropes, known as ratlines. The system secured the mast firmly, and

Tudor shipwrights using compasses to draw details of a ship's hull.

also acted as a rope ladder for sailors going aloft. These made up the standing rigging, which was permanently set.

In order for the ship to move and respond to changing winds, running rigging had to be supplied, to move the yards carrying the sails. This was a far more complex system, involving miles of rope and a variety of blocks of different sizes. The riggers needed to understand the whole system thoroughly. The use of blocks was a delicate balancing act to make the work manageable without making it too complex. The rigger had to be master of a whole range of skills, including all kinds of splicing and knotting, but his main asset was a clear understanding of how a ship works. It was a job that demanded experience and the ability to deal with intricate systems. It also called for a very good head for heights, as some of the work inevitably had to be done at the top of a tall mast or out at the end of a yardarm. Safety harnesses were unknown, and the riggers would probably have scorned to use them. Some years ago I was fortunate enough to meet the gentleman responsible for the rigging on the *Cutty Sark*, and he made his way up the ratlines as easily as a man strolling up a staircase.

The shipyard brought together a wide range of skills, from the man with the adze to the sail maker, sewing heavy canvas and the blacksmith providing the ironwork. Everything was done by hand. Patterns of work were established in which everyone in the yard knew their places and practised their own skills. These changed little through the centuries when wooden ships ruled the seas.

The first shipyards

Apart from the obvious requirement that a shipyard has to be set at the water's edge, the other most important factor was the availability of timber. It is difficult to imagine how much wood went into the biggest ships and it is even difficult to work it out when actual figures are supplied. The standard unit of measurement was the 'load', which was simply the amount that could be pulled by one horse. Experiments in the eighteenth century suggest that, during an earlier age when roads were either non-existent or wretchedly bad, this would be about half a ton. At that time a 64-gun warship for the Navy used 2,000 loads or about 1,000 tons of timber: that is an awful lot of trees. We get a glimpse of the problem in the accounts of the *Great Michael* built on the east coast of Scotland and launched in 1506. This was an immense vessel, 240ft (73m) overall and 36ft (11m) beam. By this time ships were already carrying an array of cannon, whether they were naval vessels or merchantmen, and to keep the ship afloat under bombardment, the wooden walls were 10ft (3m) thick. The job was so big that it was said that by the time it was completed there was not an oak tree left standing in Fife and extra wood had to be imported from Norway. Reading stories such as this it is easy to understand why the presence of woodland was as important as deep water when siting a yard.

When we think of shipyards today we tend to imagine a complex of sheds and dry docks overlooked by towering cranes. Early yards were far simpler. The slipways were little more than inlets scooped out of the bank of a tidal river and lined with timbers. On these, the ships were constructed in the open air. There might be a few simple buildings for sail making and other crafts, but in general the site would be dominated by the gradually growing hull of the ship, surrounded by great piles of maturing timber. Shipbuilding was a slow process: timber needed years to mature so that the wood that was used for a ship would probably have been cut before the first plans were even drawn. Not surprisingly, little remains of the vast number of small yards that could once have been found all round the British coast. It is often difficult to imagine now, but many of our seaside towns, long since given over to tourism, were once major centres of the industry. Scarborough, for example, was far more important in the seventeeth century than Newcastle. The quiet town of Barnstaple was building ships at least as early as the fifteenth century, with the first recorded launch taking place in 1434. This modest town supplied five of the ships that joined Drake's fleet that defeated the Spanish Armada. Visit these towns today, and there are few traces of this aspect of their history. There is one survivor from those times, however, which really allows one to recapture a sense of the past.

In 1709 the Duke of Montagu had ambitious plans for importing produce from St Lucia in the West Indies. He sent out an expedition and began creating a port on the Beaulieu River in Hampshire. Unfortunately, by the time the expedition had crossed the Atlantic, St Lucia had been taken over by the French. There was no trade for the new Montagu Town, so it needed another use: it became a shipbuilding centre. As it turned out, the plans worked very well. There was a broad main street, bordered by brick houses, leading down to the water's edge. This was ideal for moving loads of timber from the nearby New Forest, and the houses intended for dockers and merchants could do just as well for shipbuilders. The name Montagu Town was lost and it became Buckler's Hard. It is a very modest place, yet it was here in the eighteenth century that some of the great ships of the Royal Navy were built, including *Agamemnon*, which was commanded for a time by Horatio Nelson, and which he always described as his favourite vessel. She was a fourth-rate ship, which does not mean that she was badly constructed, but simply describes her armament. A first rate carried over a hundred guns: *Agamemnon*'s sixty-four guns put her in the fourth-rate category.

Fortunately, not only has Buckler's Hard itself been well preserved, but we also know quite a lot about what went on there. The yard was under the control of a master shipwright, and from 1747 that man was Henry Adams. He remained active right up to his death in 1805. The master shipwright needed to be a man of many talents, a combination of artist, engineer, craftsman and business organiser. He was responsible for the design of a new ship, and we can see from Adams' surviving notebooks how he went about his work. Long before any detailed plans were drawn, he sketched the vessel as he envisaged it out on the water. It was his vision that gave it shape and form. His was also the controlling force throughout construction. Even after he retired, he kept his eye on things. He lived in what is now the hotel, and he had an eyrie at the top of the house, where a telescope was mounted. Here he could overlook the works. Each workman was given a number and if Adams spotted anyone slacking or misbehaving the number was run up the flagpole and someone was in trouble. The miscreant had to climb up the ladder to receive a tongue lashing or worse from Mr Adams.

Naval dockyards

The ships were rarely, if ever, completed at Buckler's Hard. After the launch they were towed round the coast for fitting out at Portsmouth. Building for the Navy was a major part of all ship construction from medieval times, right through to the end of the eighteenth century. Britain was not always a great trading nation. During Elizabeth I's reign there were no more than twenty 200-ton vessels in the country: the rest of the mercantile fleet was trading in coastal waters. In the very important Baltic trade the Dutch at this time had around a thousand vessels: Britain had a very modest fifty-one. There was one class of vessel that was neither trader nor naval ship – the craft of the privateers who waged an unofficial war against the galleons of Spain and Portugal. They also found a shameful but lucrative new enterprise – the slave trade.

By the eighteenth century, there were other important changes within Britain that were also calling for more and more craft. Fishing fleets ventured ever further from home, out into the North Sea and the Atlantic. The development of coal mines, particularly in north-east England, bred a demand for colliers to carry fuel, especially to London. It was not a new trade – Sacoles Lane, a version of Sea Coals Lane, is recorded in London, marking the spot where coals were landed as early at 1228, but as the city grew, so did the demand. The colliers had to be sturdy vessels to withstand the poundings of the North Sea, and one of these craft was to prove its worth in waters far away from Britain's shores. The *Earl of Pembroke* was built at Whitby in 1764 for the coal trade. She was 366 tons, less than 100ft long and just under 30ft wide, so that she could scarcely be described as sleek. In 1768 she was bought by the Navy and renamed HMS *Endeavour Bark*, the 'Bark' being added because there already was another *Endeavour* in the fleet. It is just as *Endeavour* that she became famous when, under Captain James Cook, she set off in 1768 to explore Australia. A replica can be seen at Whitby, and visitors can even take a sail along the coast. In doing so, it is worth taking a moment to think what it must have been like two centuries ago, when this modest vessel was home to ninety-six men.

The merchant fleet may have been expanding, but shipbuilding was still dominated by the needs of the Navy, and it is the naval dockyards that provide most of the information that we have on how and where wooden ships were constructed – and, very importantly, we begin to find names of employees. Traditionally Alfred the Great has been called the father of the Navy, as he ordered ships to be built to fight off Norse invaders. Other kings down the centuries assembled great fleets. The first semi-official naval base was established by Richard I at Portsmouth, but it was King John who ordered the first walled dock to be built there in 1212. It was not until 1495 that a dry dock was built. It was here in 1509 that Henry VIII ordered the construction of a warship, which included a revolutionary new idea in naval warfare. The vessel was fitted with gun ports, which enabled her to fire broadsides – as wooden warships were to do for over three centuries. The actual guns placed on board had such fearsome names as 'murderer' and 'great murderer', but whether they lived up to those names is rather a different matter. The king named her after his sister *Mary Rose.* She sank thirty-six years later, but large sections of the hull and many artefacts were raised in 1982. A section of the hull is on display at Portsmouth and one can discover a great deal about construction methods at the time.

Apart from the keel, which is elm, oak was used throughout the construction, and it has been estimated that this one ship would have devoured the timber from 15 hectares of woodland. Building work would have started with the laying down of the keel. This was over a 100ft in length, far too long for a single piece of timber. It was made out of two massive bits of elm, scarfed together. After that stern and stem posts were added, together with the floor planking and a keelson, a second massive timber above the keel. The floor was held in place with iron bolts, a comparatively new material making its way into the industry. The basic shape of the vessel was then defined by the ribs and here we begin to get a glimpse into the shipwright's craft. Each rib has to be just the right shape and size, which could only be achieved by using some form of template. Traditionally, shipwrights depended on their own instinctive feel for a ship, but on a vessel of this size, such rough and ready methods would only have led to disaster. Shipbuilding was becoming more complex as the vessels grew ever bigger, and large vessels required large workforces: shipbuilding had moved from a craft to an industry.

In 1547 it was decided that Portsmouth was too far from London and the fleet was moved to the Medway and the Thames. New yards were established at Chatham, Deptford and Woolwich, of which Chatham was far and away the most important. Wage bills for 1584 show Chatham paying out £3,680 and the rest £253 between them. It is only now that individuals begin to emerge. James Baker was Henry VIII's main shipbuilder, but it was his son Matthew, who took over in 1572, who was the very first to be given the title Master Shipwright. Just as Henry Adams had done two centuries later, he made sketches of the ships he planned to build. One of the most intriguing of these shows a drawing of a fish superimposed over a warship hull. The shape of the hull, with blunt bows and narrowing down to the stern, came to be known from the drawing as 'cod's head, mackerel tail'. It was Baker who introduced the method of describing the size of a ship, what we call tonnage, but this was not originally a measure of weight at all. It was based on tunns, the number of tunns or barrels of

Bordeaux wine that could be fitted into the hull. This rather arbitrary measure eventually gave way to a measure by weight not volume – the number of tons of water displaced by the ship.

Baker not only sketched vessels, he used a method of showing the shape of the hull by drawing a series of cross-sections on boards or paper. A variety of curves could be used, but they were all based on segments of a circle. Apprentices drew these curves using compasses, giant versions of the compasses used in school geometry lessons. These drawings could be used for making templates that were taken off into the forest to choose suitable compass timber. Once work got under way, the Master Shipwright was just that – master of everything that went into construction. The work was not particularly well paid, but it offered considerable scope for corruption. In the seventeenth century the job was secured as much by influence as by merit, which was certainly the case with one of Baker's successors, the notorious Phineas Pett. He somehow managed to hold his post through a series of scandals, of which the most blatant came to light in 1608. Pett had discarded large quantities of timber as being worthless and not fit to be used for a naval craft. It turned out that he had found them good enough, however, to build a 160-ton ship for his personal profit. All that earned him was a reprimand.

During the Dutch Wars of the seventeenth century, new naval dockyards were established at Harwich and Sheerness, but the real changes followed the events of 1667. The Dutch fleet sailed up the Medway and attacked the dockyard, destroying much of the fleet. It was a major catastrophe and marked a move away from such a vulnerable position. Portsmouth, which had been neglected, was now revitalised and in 1691 work also began on a brand new dockyard on reclaimed land near Plymouth, later to be known as Devonport. This was an opportunity to incorporate all the very latest ideas on shipbuilding and ship repair. It is worth looking at in some detail, because it represented the very best practices of the day.

This was not a big site by modern standards, no more than 10 hectares, but there was a lot packed into the space. There was a wet dock able to hold two first-rate ships and a dry dock that could hold one. The wet dock was innovative. Earlier versions had all been built with timber, but this was stone with double lock gates, and was so impressive that it was known as the Great Ship Basin. Over the centuries, ever larger docks would be built on site, and by the nineteenth century the old dock was merely prosaic Number 1 Basin. Beyond that was the Great Stone Storehouse, which was exactly what the name suggests and an even more impressive 1,000ft-long ropery. Around these were a number of smaller warehouses and stores. The men responsible for running the yard were housed in an elegant terrace and there was more modest accommodation for the rest of the

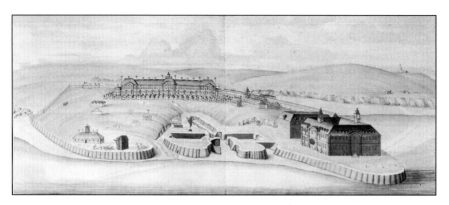

The Royal Naval Dockyard at Plymouth at the end of the seventeenth century, with the imposing terrace of officers' houses in the background.

workers. By the time the work was completed in 1698 there was a work-force of around 300. In 1694, the first ship the forty-eight-gun *Anglesey* was launched from the yard. The yard steadily grew through the years, and the next innovation was the introduction of covered slipways. No. 1 Slip, begun in 1763, was the first covered slipway in any naval dockyard, and is remarkable for its complex and very beautiful timber roof. Anyone who thinks functional buildings must necessarily be ugly should come here and have their minds changed forever.

The dockyard staff, a mixture of naval officers and civilians, was employed by the Navy Board and were organised on a strictly hierarchical basis. At the top was the Commissioner and below him the Clerk of the Cheque, who mustered the workmen and looked after the accounts, and the Clerk of the Survey or Storekeeper. Between them, with the help of a small number of clerks, they were responsible for administration. Construction and repair came under the control of the Master Shipwright, with subsidiary Masters looking after specialised trades – sail making, rigging and so on. There was also a separate Clerk of the Ropeyard. The senior officers were highly valued, and one gets a very good impression of their status from the houses that were built for them.

Working conditions

By the end of the eighteenth century, the royal dockyards employed a workforce of more than 11,000. The work at the shipyard was hard and the pay poor. In eighteenth-century Devonport the maximum pay for the elite shipwrights and caulkers was 2s 1d (roughly 10p) per day, while the boys whose job it was to unpick old ropes to make oakum for the caulkers earned just sixpence (0.5p) a day. It is, as mentioned in the Preface, always difficult to judge wages from so long ago. The pay has to be seen in the context of the times, and the wages compare reasonably well with the new jobs being created in the Industrial Revolution in other parts of Britain. The overseer of spinning in an eighteenth-century cotton mill, for example, looking after a workforce of about sixty received much the same as a ship-wright and at the opposite end of the scale the youngest workers' pay was comparable to that of the oakum boys.

Working conditions were also very similar to those in other industries. Working hours depended on daylight: dawn to dusk in winter and at least 12 hours a day in summer. There were four paid holidays a year – three full days and one half day. The men were free at Christmas and Easter, but unpaid at those times. The biggest difficulty they faced was the system of payment: they got their money quarterly in arrears. As no one had any savings, this meant that when they started work they were almost instantly in debt, and once they did get paid, all they could do was pay those debts off and start accumulating a fresh lot. The advantage for the employers is obvious: they had a captive workforce that could not afford to leave.

In other yards around the country, much material was bought in from specialists. In the south-west of England, for example, Bridport in Dorset was famous for its rope making and local forges would provide items such as anchors. The naval dockyards, however, had to be completely self-sufficient, so wherever possible everything had to be done on site. The shipwrights were responsible for construction from the laying of the keel to the completion of the upper deck. There was virtually no machinery involved and a good deal of skill was required in shaping the many curved timbers by hand. Other skilled workers included sail makers, riggers, anchor smiths and mast makers. Rope making was a vital element. A first-rate ship, such as HMS *Victory* built at Chatham in 1759, used an almost unbelievable amount of rope, 26 miles of it, and rope does not last for ever. It had constantly to be renewed. As a result the ropery was never out of business, and until the end of the century the rope was all made by hand. The process was repetitive but required concentration.

Rope at the time was made from hemp, which first has to be hackled, a process that aligns the natural fibres. The hackler grabbed a handful of hemp, applied a little oil, then pulled it through metal spikes stuck on a wooden block. Only when all the tangles had been removed and the fibres were all running together could the actual job of rope making get under way. This took place in the ropery or rope walk. The spinner had a bag of hackled hemp. He selected a few strands, twisted them together and

Although this photograph was taken c. 1900 at Porthmadog, little has changed from centuries ago. The man at the left holds a caulking hammer and the one next to him an adze.

attached them to a hook mounted on the rim of a large wheel. He repeated this until all four hooks on the wheel had been filled. Then a boy started turning the wheel, slowly and regularly, and the spinner began walking backwards down the walk, paying out the hemp strands. As he went along he laid the rope onto T-shaped supports, and continued until he got to the end of the walk. A long rope needs a long walk, hence the 1,000ft-long Plymouth ropery. At the end, the rope was detached from the hooks and put on a reel. The spinner then began walking back to the start as the rope was equally slowly wound on again. This was just to make one strand of slender cord, and many cords would have to be spun together to make ropes, and ropes combined for the heavy duty cables, such as those that held the anchors. Throughout the eighteenth century these busy yards

Riggers at work on a schooner, the Thirlmere, *at Whitehaven in the late nineteenth century.*

were hugely labour intensive. Even the big cranes depended on manpower, being operated by treadmills, a fine example of which can be seen at Harwich.

Shipwrights and apprentices

The craftsmen learned their skills as apprentices, a privilege for which a premium was paid to the master. There were no formal educational requirements. One early set of rules simply decreed that any boy was eligible provided he was over 14 years old, in good health and over 4ft 10in high. Shipbuilding was usually descried as a 'mystery', which was simply the medieval word for a craft or occupation, hence the famous Mystery Plays put on by craft guilds. But the truth is that the work of the shipwright in particular was a good deal more of a mystery than it was a science. There were no formal rules and it was in the interest of the master shipwright to keep his knowledge to himself, and when he passed any information on to the next generation he made sure that the secrecy was preserved. One apprentice who was signed up in 1787 paid £3 to the master at the start of his tuition in 'ship drafting' and another £3 'when I can lay a draft by my self'. But if the apprentice tried to pass on his knowledge to anyone else he had to pay a £10 fine. That was a considerable sum of money – four months' wages for a qualified shipwright. The teaching was all practical and indeed there was no accepted theory. Individual shipwrights really did keep their very own mysteries. It was not really very satisfactory. As a writer in the influential *Nautical Mirror* noted, looking back on those days from the middle of the nineteenth century: 'work was done at the arbitrary pleasure of the builder, by his individual caprice or conjecture'.

One of the most complete descriptions that we have of one of the great naval yards of the eighteenth century was written by Daniel Defoe. He is best known as the author of *Robinson Crusoe*, but he was also an indefatigable traveller around Britain, recording what he saw in great detail. Between 1724 and 1726 he published his account of *A Tour through the Whole Island of Great Britain* and one place that impressed him greatly was the Chatham dockyard, at that time still 'the chief arsenal of the royal navy'. It is worth quoting at length.

> The buildings here are indeed like the ships themselves, surprisingly large, and in their several kinds beautiful: The ware-houses, or rather streets of ware-houses, and store-houses for laying up the naval treasure are the largest in dimension, and the most in number, that are any where to be seen in the world: The rope-walk for making cables, and the forges for anchors and other iron-work, bear a proportion to the rest; as also the wet-dock for keeping masts, and yards of the greatest size, where they lye sunk in the water to preserve them, the boat-yard, the anchor yard; all like the whole, monstrously great and extensive.

He then went on to list the stores needed for the ships, in what seems to have been a nautical Aladdin's cave.

> For this purpose there are separate and respective magazines of pitch, tarr, hemp, flax, tow, rosin, oyl, tallow; also of sail cloth, canvas, anchors, cables, standing and running rigging, ready fitted, and cordage not fitted; with all kinds of ship-chandlery necessaries and gunners stores, and also anchors of all sizes, grapnells, chains, bolts, and spikes, wrought and unwrought iron, cast-iron work, such as potts, caldrons, furnaces, &c. also boats, spare-masts, and yards; with a great quantity of lead and nails, and other necessaries

(too many to be enumerated) whose store looks as if it were inexhaustible.

Probably the best chance to get an idea of what a naval yard of the eighteenth century actually looked like is to visit the National Maritime Museum in Greenwich to see the dockyard models. These were commissioned for George III by Lord Sandwich between 1773 and 1774. They not only show an overall view of the yards, but also ships in different stages of construction, and lots of details about the technology in use.

Private shipyards

There were no yards of anything like this size and complexity providing ships for the merchant fleet at this time. The firm founded by John Scott at Greenock in 1711 on the Clyde can be taken as a typical example of a medium-sized yard that was to grow steadily over the years. At first it specialised in herring busses, small but sturdy fishing vessels, worked by a four-man crew. Records from 1728 show that there were around 900 of these vessels working out of Greenock. Things began to change in the 1750s when larger vessels were being built for the newly developed Greenland whaling trade. A notable event in the history of Scott's came in 1756 when it built a large square-rigged merchantman for Hull, the very first ship to be built on the Clyde for owners outside Scotland. Most of the work continued to be in building comparatively small vessels: of the six built in 1776, for example, the largest was 77 tons. Nevertheless, the yard was steadily extended, with the addition of a graving dock for ship repairs. By the end of the eighteenth century, there was a considerable trade between the Clyde and North America, but nearly all the ships were being built in America, where there were huge timber supplies. The Scottish yards were also hampered by the high prices they had to pay for English oak. Things only really began to change at the very end of the century, when Scott's built two vessels, the 600-ton *Brunswick* for the Nova Scotia trade and the 650-ton *Caledonia* for transporting timber for the Navy yards. This increased activity was reflected in the general expansion of Greenock as a whole from an estimated population of under 1,500 in 1700 to nearly 20,000 a century later.

The changes to yards such as Scott's were substantial and real: what did not alter was the method of working. Throughout the eighteenth century in Britain, the average size of merchantman only increased from 80 to 100 tons, and there was very little development in the mechanics of the ship. At the start of the eighteenth century, it was generally reckoned that a vessel would need one crew man for every 10 tons and a hundred years later it had only improved to 1 in 13 tons. This was a very conservative industry as a check on the patents for shipbuilding reveals – practically the only innovations recorded were for improved pumps. The problem was partly endemic to an industry with a craft tradition that had changed very little in either organisation or technology. It was also an industry with little incentive to change. Apart from the trade to the West Indies and North America, dominated by American ships, the East India trade was controlled by the East India Company, who built their own vessels mostly in India. Scott's was a small yard compared with the naval yards, but by the end of the eighteenth century stood comparison with the other main shipbuilding centres of London and Bristol. It was to continue as a highly successful company well into the twentieth century, but merged with Lithgows Ltd to become Scott Lithgow in 1967. Shipbuilding finally came to an end in 1986, 275 years after the first keel was laid.

Naval dockyard archives

Given the dominance of the naval dockyards, it is no surprise to find that their records are far easier to trace than those for private shipyards. The main records are kept in the National Archives. Until 1832 the dockyards were controlled by the Navy Board, which, although it was officially subordinate to the Admiralty, was largely independent in practice. There are certain complications in that men who finished their apprenticeships to become dockyard shipwrights might then sign on as ships' carpenters and at a later date might return to the shipyard. In trying to trace skilled artificers and tradesmen it may be necessary to consult both the Navy Board and Admiralty records. These records are far from complete for the different dockyards, particularly for the early years. The most important are the Yard Pay Books. There are separate categories covering different trades: shipwrights, caulkers, coopers and rope makers. There are also records of artificers who have been dismissed, not perhaps where one would most wish to find an ancestor's name. During the Napoleonic Wars, press gangs operated at all Britain's seaports, whisking away anyone with experience of seamanship – and sometimes even if they had never set foot on a ship – to serve in the Navy. It was obviously essential that trained shipyard staff remained in the yards, to build the new ships that were needed and to repair those damaged in action. There are substantial records of Protection from the Press, listing the men who were exempt from naval service.

The records vary greatly for different yards. At Deptford, for example, the records for sawyers cover a period from 1765 to 1803, while the

Chatham records for the ropeyard go all the way back to 1660. A catalogue is available online at www.nationalarchives.gov.uk; click on Research Guide A to Z and then go to Royal Naval Dockyards. There are also a number of records held at the National Maritime Museum, Greenwich, which contain some interesting information about the yards, but are in general less helpful in providing information on personnel. These records are more likely to be of interest in providing further information once you have already established a connection with a particular yard. There are a number of helpful guides to be found online at www.nmm.ac.uk /researchers/library/research-guides. The guides A2 and A3 are the most useful for family historians.

Finding details of private shipyards before 1800 is an altogether more difficult problem. Nearly all the yards whose documents have been preserved in the archives listed in the previous chapter were established in the nineteenth and twentieth centuries. Even the few that were started earlier have virtually nothing relating to the first decades of their existence. You will have to look to different sources for information on this.

Apprenticeship records

The most useful starting point is to search for records of apprenticeships. Indentures were private documents, but from 1710 to 1810 they were taxed, and as a result were recorded in a central register. This has been indexed and the index can be consulted at the Society of Genealogists' Guildhall Library in London. The documents will usually have the name of the apprentice, the name of the master and his trade, the amount paid to the master, and the name of the apprentice's father. Most of the originals are held in County Record Offices. The apprentice records can also be tracked back through Guild records. The Tyne and Wear Archives, for example, has lists of the apprentices to the Company of Shipwrights of Newcastle upon Tyne, dating back to 1613, and for the Incorporated Company of Sail Makers from 1662. This information can lead, in turn, to the discovery of a great deal of data about a local shipbuilder, even when the business papers of the concern have all disappeared. The City Archives in Hull, for example, reveal a very interesting story. The Blaydes family of Hull (Blaides in earlier documents) were shipbuilders in Hull from around 1630 to the end of the eighteenth century, during which time they employed about a hundred apprentices. They built a number of ships for the Royal Navy, including the *Bounty*, famous for the mutiny when William Bligh was captain. Some of the records provide remarkably useful information. The Newcastle upon Tyne apprentice lists not only give the name but also the town where they lived and the father's name and occupation. In the earliest records, however, many of the occupations simply appear under the rather general title of yeoman.

Manorial records

Records are easiest to track down when they relate to established ship-building centres, but there were small concerns spread right around the coast, which would seem to have left little or no trace of their existence. We do know, however, that some of these enterprises will be likely to feature in manorial records. The manor lay at the heart of the feudal system, introduced by the Normans. The lord of the manor would retain some of the land he controlled for his own use, usually the most profitable parts, while the rest would be let out to tenants. These could pay rent in cash or kind, and could be required to work on the lord's estate and could be called on for military service. This system required administration and that inevitably meant documentation. The most important documents are the surveys, listing the tenants and the terms on which they held the land. In most cases there would also be an indication of whether or not the tenant was a freeman. Some of these documents also contain maps, which can give valuable information about the way in which the land was used. Terriers or extants described the lands belonging to a manor. Rentals or rent rolls are just what the names suggest. Court rolls describe the proceedings of the courts that dealt with disputes between the lord and his tenants and also record other facts, including the deaths of tenants and the remarriage of widows. Custumals documented rents and services due to the lord as well as manorial customs.

One of the important resources in the manor was woodland and for centuries shipbuilders would have had to treat with the lord to acquire the timber for their ships. So even if the lord was not himself directly concerned with the industry he would most certainly profit from any local activity, so there is a chance of discovering information in the documents. Even as late as the eighteenth century, one still finds records of shipyards purchasing their timber from manorial estates. Having said this, it remains true that the chances of finding hard facts about distant ancestors in ship-building through these sources are not high. The main reason being that because these are private not public documents, only a fraction of the whole has survived. But if you have managed to trace your ancestry as far back as you can using the various sources mentioned above, it is well worth the effort.

The first thing you need to know is the name of the manor in which you are interested. Manors came in all kinds of sizes, the largest encompassing several villages, and many had names that are no longer in use. A useful starting point is the Victoria History of the Counties of England, where it is easy to relate the name of the modern village or town to the medieval manor. Most local reference libraries will have copies for the immediate area. The next stage is to discover whether records have survived. Documents are listed in the Manorial Documents Register, maintained by the National Archives. It is gradually being made available online at www.mdr.nationalarchives.gov.uk. At the time of writing, the areas of interest for shipbuilding that are available are: Hampshire, the Isle of Wight, Lancashire, Yorkshire, parts of Cumbria and all of Wales.

Tracking down the relevant documents is, for most of us, only the start of the problem. All the early documents are in Latin, often rather badly written and make use of abbreviations. Most people, and that certainly includes the author, will find them as intelligible as documents written in Chinese. If you think that there really is information you need in early manorial documents, then you will probably have to pay for a professional to translate them for you. If you are able to trace your family back this far, then you will have been extremely fortunate. But we are now going to move forward again in time to a period where research is a good deal easier.

Chapter Three

A TIME OF CHANGE

*Mechanisation – Naval dockyard workers –
New construction techniques –
Early steamer development – Brunel's ships –
Iron steamship construction –
The first trade unions – Trade directories – Newspapers –
Early union documents – Preserved ships*

Mechanisation

The eighteenth century saw the Industrial Revolution sweep through Britain, transforming industry after industry, but at first scarcely touching the world of shipbuilding. New materials were introduced. Wooden ships had been plagued by *teredo navalis* the ship worm, not a worm at all but a mollusc that bored into the wood below the waterline, riddling the hull with holes. It has been said that the worm was responsible for the loss of more ships in the eighteenth century than war and weather combined. All kinds of different coatings had been tried to keep the beast at bay, including the unlikely notion of covering the hull in brown paper. Eventually a permanent solution was found by attaching thin sheets of copper to the hull. This was so successful that 'copper bottomed' came into the language to indicate complete safety and security. It was not only materials that were being introduced to the dockyards.

The first important invention to bring change to the dockyard was the mechanisation of the rope walk. The main improvements were the work of two brothers, Edward and William Chapman. Edward was the manager of a rope works near Newcastle upon Tyne and William an engineer who was later to become one of the pioneers in developing steam locomotives. In essence, the walking man of the old ropery was replaced with a machine mounted on a railed track. Not only was it more efficient, but it also enabled rope to be laid with great accuracy as it was run at a constant speed. A more developed version of the Chapmans' machine can be seen at the rope walk at Chatham. Regular demonstrations are given, and it is a mesmerising sight, seeing the strands come together and twist into a rope as the carriage trundles down its quarter-mile-long track.

The deep conservatism of the Admiralty and the Navy Board was a major factor in preventing innovation. The world of factories was being transformed, with work that had once been done by hand in cottages and small workshops being performed by machines in factories. In the shipyards things went on as they had done for centuries. The first real signs of change came with the appointment of Samuel Bentham to the post of Inspector-General for the naval dockyards in 1796. Although he had come from a wealthy family, he still served a full apprenticeship as a shipwright. He travelled widely in Europe and spent ten years in Russia where he introduced a whole range of new ideas into their national shipbuilding industry. He did the same in Britain, but also set himself the task of fighting the corruption and nepotism that was rife in the dockyards, a campaign that made him more enemies than friends. He was desperate to increase efficiency and was one of the very few in that closed world who regarded innovation as a benefit rather than something to be avoided wherever possible. It was at this time that he met and made friends with a brilliant French engineer who had fled the Revolution, Marc Brunel.

Brunel had invented a series of machines for making blocks. It was estimated that in wartime the Admiralty would need 70,000 blocks a year, and each of them was made individually with only the simplest machinery. Brunel's idea was radical. He broke down the production of blocks into its component parts and devised a machine for each specific component. The pieces would then be brought together for assembly. The idea was welcomed by Bentham but was met with reluctance elsewhere and might never have been accepted but for an accident. A fire destroyed the Navy's entire stock of blocks at Portsmouth. Something had to be done and Brunel was authorised to install machinery in a new building at the dockyard. The actual manufacture of the blockmaking machines was undertaken by another great engineer, Henry Maudsley. Between 1802 and 1806, forty-five machines were installed, some of which were comparatively straightforward, such as drilling and sawing devices, but others were far more ingenious. Once a block had been roughed out, it needed to be given a smooth, curved shape and this was the job of the shaping machine that could handle ten blocks at the same time. When the block mill was fully at work 10 men could turn out 140,000 blocks a year. This would have required at least a hundred men before, and there was the

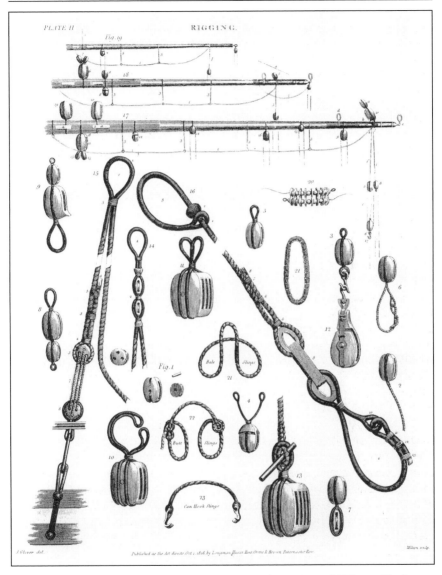

An illustration from Rees's Cyclopaedia *shows the variety of different blocks and dead-eyes that could be found on a sailing ship.*

extra advantage that the blocks were standardised, accurate and all made on the one site.

The Navy did little to help Brunel. On the contrary, he was constantly hindered in his work. He had spent his own money designing the machines

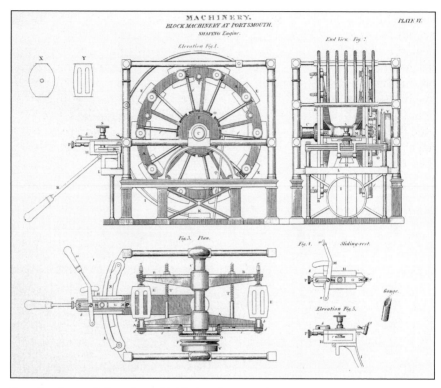

Details of one of Marc Brunel's blockmaking machines. This is the shaping machine.

and constructing the prototypes, but had the greatest difficulty in getting paid. Matters became even worse when a new man, Mr Burr, was placed over him at the block mills. Burr was illiterate and had no experience of working machinery. Brunel had begun by carefully training up operatives to work the new machines. Burr's first action was to employ fifteen boys to work the machines and he refused to allow time for proper training. The result was that the workforce at the mills was greatly increased – and production went down dramatically. It was all too symptomatic of the attitudes of those who controlled the dockyards at this time. Brunel left the dockyard, wholly disillusioned in his dealings with the Admiralty, an attitude he passed on to his even more famous son, Isambard Kingdom Brunel, who later wrote of the Admiralty: 'they have an unlimited supply of *some negative* principle which seems to absorb and eliminate everything that approaches them'.

The Portsmouth block mills still stand, and some of the machines can be seen in the dockyard museum at Portsmouth and there are others in the

Science Museum, London. It is easy to see that they are beautifully made, even if they are no longer demonstrated. They represent something quite new in the world of manufacture: they were arguably the very first to use the technology of mass production. This was a huge step forward in productivity, but it also marked a radical change in the workforce – more machines meant fewer men. What made economic sense for the Navy Board could prove an economic disaster for the individual. There was very little the men could do – relations between employers and employees in the naval dockyards were no better at the beginning of the nineteenth century than they had been for all the preceding years.

Naval dockyard workers

The quarterly payment system lasted right up to 1814, though the Navy Board did set up a Subsistence Allowance, a scheme for providing the men with official, interest-free loans, instead of forcing them into the hands of the loan sharks. There was, however, a slow move towards 'task' payments for shipbuilders working on new craft, which was a form of piece work. The trouble was that the men could never work out what the rates for the job were supposed to be, and the system was often little more than an attempt to disguise an actual drop in pay. In 1801, at a time of declining food supplies, matched by rising prices, new low task rates were introduced at Devonport. The result was a riot. The Admiralty stores were attacked and the food sold off cheaply to the townspeople of Plymouth. The Town Commissioner tried to read the Riot Act, but was bombarded by the citizens and scurried off before he had uttered a single word. Eventually the authorities had to admit defeat and agreed to remove the cuts. It can hardly be described as good management when the only method available for negotiation is the riot. In this, as in so much else, the authorities showed themselves reluctant to take on change. Sometimes, however, there was no alternative: the new had to be accepted.

New construction techniques

One of the major developments of the Industrial Revolution came with changes in the production of iron, which poured from the new generation of blast furnaces in ever greater quantities. It arrived just in time as far as shipbuilding was concerned, as there were now serious worries about the diminishing supplies of suitable timber. The curved compass timber was particularly scarce, and this was essential for the knees that were a vital part of the whole structure. HMS *Victory*, for example, has 438 of them in her hull, but it was not until the beginning of the nineteenth century that Thomas Roberts of the Navy Office came up with the idea of replacing wood with iron. It seems obvious, but it was considered such a brilliant and revolutionary idea at the time that in 1807 he was awarded £800 by the King's Order in Council and a silver medal from the Society of Arts. Iron strapping was also used to strengthen the hull. The results of this advance can be seen in the frigate HMS *Unicorn*, launched at Chatham in 1824 and now preserved in Dundee. She was built for war, but was launched in a time of peace and was never fitted out for sailing, which is one reason why the hull has been so well preserved. She was 'mothballed', covered with a roof for protection.

Early steamer development

Externally, *Unicorn* looks no different from any other ship of the time and she was built to work under sail. Yet throughout Britain, at the time she was launched, steam engines were puffing away, working machinery in

The gun deck of HMS Unicorn: *the iron knees can be clearly seen between the gun ports.*

mills and factories, pumping water from mines and trundling along the first primitive railways. Steam had even been used to power Brunel's blockmaking machines. The idea of using steam power to move a ship was still, however, in its infancy. The first practical steam engines had been limited to working as pumps, but thanks to the work of James Watt in the 1760s they were able to produce rotary motion. The obvious use in ships was to try and harness this power to turn a paddle wheel. The first successful trial was the work of a French aristocrat, Marquis de Jouffroy d'Abbans. His steamer *Pyroscaphe* set off down the River Saône in 1783. It could have given France a world lead in a new industry, if the whole country had not been plunged into the social turmoil of revolution. As it was the movement for innovation moved to Britain and America.

The first British experiment was the work of the Scottish engineer William Symington. He was born in the lead-mining district of Lanarkshire, and his first experience with steam came when he built an engine to drain the mine at Wanlockhead. In 1788 he designed a tiny engine, had it made by a local brass founder, and then installed it in a boat. He had something of a problem, since most steam-engine development was forbidden under a patent given to James Watt. He tried to get round this by going back to an earlier idea, the atmospheric engine, first developed by Thomas Newcomen nearly a century earlier. In these engines, the top of the cylinder was open, and contained a piston suspended from one end of a pivoted beam. Steam was admitted below the piston and then condensed creating a vacuum. Air pressure then drove the piston down, lifting pump rods hung from the opposite end of the beam. Once pressure was equalised, the weight of pump rods pulled that end of the beam down again, raising the piston so that the whole process could begin again. Symington managed to produce the up and down motion of the piston by having two cylinders with the pistons working out of phase – the force of one going down pulling the other up. The first trial took place on Dalswinton Loch and the vessel chugged along at a respectable 5 miles per hour. Attempts to build on this initial success faltered for a variety of reasons, including threats of legal action by Boulton & Watt, claiming infringement of Watt's patent. It was not until 1802, when Watt's patent had expired, that Symington was able to try out a more conventional steam engine in a practical, working vessel.

The *Charlotte Dundas* was designed as a tug for use on the Forth & Clyde Canal and in the first full trial on 28 March 1803 she pulled two fully laden 70-ton barges along 20 miles of the waterway. From that point of view, the experiment was a success, but the canal proprietors were worried that the wash would damage the banks and never developed the idea any further. Shortly afterwards the first commercial steamboat service was begun on the Hudson River in America, but Britain had to wait a little longer for the next stage of development.

Henry Bell, a hotel proprietor from Helensburgh, was a friend of the Napier family who had a forge and foundry, first at Dumbarton then at Glasgow. Bell hit on the idea of building a paddle steamer for use on the Clyde and he gave the youngest of the family, David Napier, the job of casting the engine and building the boiler. It was the boiler that caused Napier the most trouble. At first he tried using cast iron and when that didn't work turned to wrought iron. Even then it leaked under pressure and Napier turned, in his own words, to 'a liberal supply of horse dung' to keep it steam tight. Named *Comet*, the vessel itself was built by John Robertson of Glasgow. The engine was quite small, with a 12½in (32cm) diameter cylinder that developed a very modest 4 horsepower. Not surprisingly she was often helped on her way by means of a square sail hoisted to the tall funnel. She was, however, a great success, and marked the start of a period of paddle-steamer construction in Scotland, in which David Napier was to play a leading role. He began by establishing a new works for building engines and boilers for ships, but soon moved on to building his own ship as well. The *Rob Roy* set off on its maiden voyage from Glasgow to Dublin in 1818 and among the passengers was Charles McIntosh, famous for devising the raincoat that bore his name. He must have needed some persuasion as he told Napier that he was sure they would all be drowned. No such calamity occurred.

The problems with early steamers were not easy to overcome. Boilers were only designed to produce steam at a very low pressure, so if you wanted more power you had to build a bigger engine. Bigger engines needed more space and more fuel, so more and more of the hull could be taken up with machinery instead of passengers or cargo. Napier was among the pioneers who tried to improve design. One of his ideas came to him after he had gone to bed. He promptly got up, went down to the dining room, rolled back the carpet and chalked his plan on the floor. Next day he copied it and took the plans to a pattern maker to begin the process of turning the inspiration into reality. The result was the so-called steeple engine. It had two vertical cylinders in line with an overhead crankshaft. Each cylinder was connected to piston rods and crossheads, which were so high that they actually poked through the deck – hence the name 'steeple'. But the steeple was not taking up valuable space below decks. The engines became very popular with Clyde shipbuilders. It still did not solve the size problem.

By the middle of the nineteenth century, boiler pressures in railway loco-motives had been raised beyond the 100lb per sq in (psi) mark, but shipbuilders did not follow suit. It was considered quite adventurous to

Scott's of Greenock in 1818. The sailing ship Christian *towers above a small paddle steamer.*

exceed a modest 15psi, and as a result engines had to be enormous with cylinders over 7ft in diameter. That was only a part of the problem. These engines were very inefficient, so that coal consumption could be as much as 20 tons a day. It was figures such as these that convinced many that steamers would never be able to work on long-distance routes. One of the alleged experts was Dr Dionysius Lardner, who 'proved' at a meeting of the British Association that no steamer could ever carry enough coal for a transatlantic crossing and still make a profit. Dr Lardner had an excellent track record of proving that things would be impossible. He calculated that if a Great Western Railway locomotive travelling through the Box tunnel suffered a brake failure it would reach a speed of 120mph, and the passengers would be unable to breathe and would all die. On that occasion the GWR's chief engineer Isambard Kingdom Brunel was able to prove him wrong: he was about to do the same again for the transatlantic passenger steamer.

Brunel's ships

There is a story that may or may not be true but which certainly fits Brunel's character. Some cautious members of the Board of the Great

Western Railway doubted the feasibility of building a railway that would stretch all the way from London to Bristol. Brunel's reply was simple – why stop there, why not go on to New York? Perhaps it was no more than bravado, but it was taken seriously by one member, Thomas Guppy. That was all the encouragement Brunel needed: he promptly set about the problem of how to build a viable transatlantic steamer. How could he overcome the old problem of finding space for both an engine and the fuel? He spotted the factor that Dr Lardner had overlooked. A floating ship has all its weight borne by the water. To move it forward all you need to do is overcome water resistance. Water resistance is dependent on the area of the hull pushing the water aside, which can be expressed in terms of surface area. But the capacity of a ship depends on its volume. If, for simplicity, you take a cube with 1m sides, and push it through water, then the area of the advancing face is $1m^2$ and the volume is $1m^3$. If you double the dimensions, the face area becomes $4m^2$, but the volume is now $8m^3$. Capacity increases at a greater rate than surface resistance. The answer to transatlantic travel was now comparatively simple: build a bigger ship. Brunel set out to design a very big ship indeed, the *Great Western*. She was to be a 1,340 ton ship, moved by paddle wheels, turned by an engine working at the very low pressure of 5psi.

Building a large steamer is not the same as building a large sailing ship. In the latter, the wooden frame is expected to give as it meets the waves, but a steam engine needs a solid base. Brunel used the technology we have already met in HMS *Unicorn*, using metal knees and iron bracing to make the hull as rigid as possible. It was Brunel's dream that the *Great Western* would be the very first ship to cross the Atlantic using steam all the way, but he was to be thwarted. She was ready to leave Bristol on 8 April 1837, but a much smaller vessel the *Sirius* had already set off from Cork four days earlier. The *Great Western* gained on her diminutive rival all the way across, but never quite made up the difference. *Sirius* was first to New York, but had scarcely a shovelful of coal left in the bunkers. Brunel's ship arrived with 200 tons left unused. Brunel may have lost the race but he had won the argument: the future lay with big ships.

Brunel now began work on a second, even more ambitious vessel, which was provisionally known as the *City of New York* and the Bristol papers reported the arrival of a large cargo of African oak, ready for work to start, but Brunel was beginning to have other ideas. He was concerned about the limitations imposed by building in timber. If he was going to increase substantially the size of ocean-going steamers, then he would soon reach a point where he could advance no further. He needed a quite new type of hull: he needed to build in iron. The technology was already available.

The new blast furnaces turned out huge amounts of cast iron, but the metal is brittle and easily broken under tension, not at all suitable for the curved metal plates that would be needed to construct a ship's hull. But in 1784, Henry Cort, working at his small iron works in Hampshire, devised a method for converting cast iron into malleable wrought iron. Equally importantly, he invented a system for squeezing white-hot ingots of iron between rollers to create flat sheets of metal. Further north in Shropshire another ironmaster, John Wilkinson, was busily improving the furnaces by introducing a steam engine to boost the blast of air. Increased efficiency meant increased output. He relied on the River Severn and its canal connections for transport to reach his customers, and in 1787 he launched a revolutionary vessel, a barge constructed out of iron. It was a success and as he wrote 'convinced the unbelievers, who were 999 in a thousand'. A barge on a river is not subjected to the same forces as a ship at sea, but it was only a question of time before the next step was taken. Charles Manby had taken out a patent for an iron steamboat, and he received an order for a vessel from France. His works were in the heart of Britain on the Birmingham canal system, so the vessel the *Aaron Manby* had to be made in sections and sent down to London. Once assembled she set off under steam down the Thames in 1822 and crossed the Channel to Le Havre.

William Laird came to Merseyside from Scotland in 1810 to try and drum up business for his father's rope works at Greenock. But he stayed on and began to plan for a new port across the water from Liverpool. That came to nothing, but he did establish the Birkenhead Iron Works, around which he laid out a new model town. He was the first shipbuilder to set up in business specifically to construct iron ships. There was thought to be a problem because of the need to navigate by magnetic compass, and it was assumed that the iron would throw everything into chaos. But the magnetism of the ship's hull is a constant, so it is possible to compensate for it, usually by placing two iron balls, one each side of the compass housing. Laird's first ship was launched in 1829, and in October 1838 their Channel packet the *Rainbow* steamed into Bristol. One of Brunel's associates, former naval Captain Christopher Claxton, went on board and was hugely impressed. He spelt out the advantages in his report: 'An average thickness of 2ft. of timber would be replaced by average thickness of 2½in. of iron, with far better ties, a more compact framework and greater strength, than wood can under any circumstance'.

Plans for the wooden *City of New York* were scrapped and replaced by new designs for the iron *Great Britain*. Once construction began everyone could see that it was not only the old plans that had been jettisoned: a whole new method of construction was to be used. In a wooden ship, the essential rigidity was supplied by the massive keel and the ribs and beams built up above it. The new ship was very different. The base was constructed from ten girders running from stem to stern, with an iron deck attached on top. Above that were five watertight transverse bulkheads and two longitudinal bulkheads, which together made a set of rigid boxes. The main problem with the hull construction was the inability of the iron works to provide large plates of iron. The best that could be done was a modest 6ft in length. These could be laid end to end along the fore and aft line, but for added strength, the individual rows were overlapped: it was the iron equivalent of a clinker-built ship.

The original intention was to follow the precedent of the *Great Western* and have immense paddle wheels to drive the ship. The job of engine design went to a young man, Francis Humphreys, and it called for a crank-shaft of unprecedented size. Existing forges used pivoted hammers, usually powered by water wheels, which imitated the action of a black-smith's arm as he hammered metal on his anvil. But there was a limit to how high the hammer head could rise, and none had a big enough gap to forge Humphreys' crankshaft. He put the problem to the manufacturer James Nasmyth who recorded how, within half an hour of receiving the letter, 'I had the whole contrivance in all its executant details, before me in the page of my Scheme Book'. What Nasmyth had sketched was a hammer head, fixed in a rigid frame, above the anvil. It was raised to the top by steam pressure and then allowed to fall back under gravity. He had designed the first steam hammer. This is an interesting example of how, now that shipbuilding was entering a new era, new technologies had to be developed in other industries.

Humphreys' delight that his problem had been solved was short-lived. Unknown to him, another new idea was being tried out by a farmer in Kent, Francis Pettit Smith. As a boy he had enjoyed playing with toy boats on the duck pond and in devising ways of moving them through the water. You can think of the paddle wheel as a water wheel in reverse: instead of water turning the wheel, the steam engine rotates the wheel and it moves the water backwards. An alternative device for moving water had been known since antiquity, the screw designed by Archimedes. When it was used for raising water the Archimedean screw was generally made as a long spiral, moving in a cylinder. Smith removed the cylinder and kept the long spiral, but it was only when the screw was accidentally broken that Smith discovered to his surprise that it worked better. He patented screw propulsion and soon moved from clockwork models on the duck pond to a full-scale trial in a small launch, the *Francis Smith*. After that he moved to an even grander vessel, a schooner that was refitted and renamed *Archimedes*. It too arrived in Bristol and so impressed Brunel and his associates that they hired it for full trials, at the end of which the paddle wheels went the way of the wooden hull. Poor Humphreys' dreams of

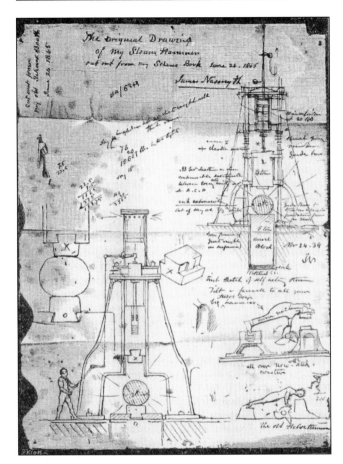

James Nasmyth's original 1839 sketch for his steam hammer.

engineering fame were ended. His engine was scrapped and a new engine constructed to drive a propeller. The SS *Great Britain* is arguably the most important ship built in the nineteenth century, thanks to the combination of iron hull and screw propeller. The one disappointment is the typically large, low-pressure steam engine, driving the shaft through a clumsy chain arrangement. In every other way it represented the future. The ship can still be seen in the Bristol dock where she was built, having been brought back home for restoration from what had once seemed likely to have been her final resting place, rusting away in the Falkland Islands.

Brunel moved on to an altogether more grandiose scheme, building the world's biggest ship, the *Great Eastern*, which never really fulfilled its promise. It was typical of the man that he would always want to do something newer and bigger than everyone else, whether it was building a

Isambard Kingdom Brunel's SS Great Britain *under construction at Bristol.*

broad-gauge railway or a monstrous ship. Others took note of the advances, but looked more closely at the commercial implications. David Napier had moved his works and let his old site to his cousin Robert Napier. In March 1839 Robert mentioned in a letter that he had met a gentleman called Cunard from Nova Scotia and had agreed to build three steamers for him that would carry the mail between Britain and Canada. This was to be the start of one of the greatest enterprises in Britain's maritime history.

Iron steamship construction

The significance of the development of the iron steamship in the history of shipbuilding cannot be overestimated. It changed everything. The centuries of slow change and established tradition were ended. New men with new ideas were arriving with quite different ways of working. Where once the shipwright had been all important, the engineer was now usurping his place. Craftsmen who prided themselves on their skills in working wood to create the intricate shapes of a hull found themselves replaced by men they sarcastically referred to as metal bashers. The job of the riveter did require skills, but these had nothing to do with the old techniques, learned through the long years of apprenticeship.

The plates that made up a ship's hull would arrive at the yard from the foundry, and then had to be cleaned, cut to size and drilled for riveting. The platers then took the plates to the skeletal frame on the slipway and positioned them. They would either be butt lapped, overlapping each other, or strapped, where the plates were fastened together by a third plate. Then the riveters moved in. The rivets themselves were simple metal bolts with a head at one end. They were heated on site in a brazier by the rivet boy, then thrown to the holder-up. He caught a rivet, inserted it and held it in place with a heavy hammer. Two riveters on the opposite side of the plate then hammered over the protruding end of the rivet, flush against the plate to hold it firm. It called for speed and accuracy as the whole job had to be completed while the rivet was still hot. The clamour of the riveters resounded throughout the iron hull and it is no surprise to find that deafness was a common complaint among shipyard workers.

Just as in the days of wooden ships the riggers and sail makers were doing very different work from the shipwrights and carpenters, so too the men who built the power units for steamers needed very different skills from those of the platers and riveters. These were men who had far more in common with the builders of locomotives and mill engines than they did with seafaring traditions. They were very much part of the new generation of engineers who had grown up with the Industrial Revolution. Perhaps the greatest difference was the need for precision. An extra 6in on the end of a mast will make little difference to how a ship performs: an error of a fraction of an inch in a steam cylinder could make the difference between efficiency and near disaster. The designers of steam engines were skilled engineers whose plans were converted into working drawings by draughtsmen. It was a world away from the old shipwright with his compasses and chalks.

The basic parts of the engine had to be cast in metal, but before that could be done a pattern had to be made in wood. The pattern maker had to have all the skill of a first-rate carpenter and needed to work to within precisely defined limits. Once completed, the pattern was set into a mould and packed with special sand. The pattern was then removed, leaving its shape retained as a hollow area in the sand that would then be filled with metal. The foundry was a place of extreme noise and heat and not a little danger, as the white-hot molten metal was poured from giant ladles into the moulds. A foundry at work was and is a dramatic sight. The furnaces belch out smoke and flame, the molten metal flows like volcanic lava amid a fire-work display of sparks. You feel the heat everywhere, but right up next to the furnace when it is being tapped, the heat is almost literally blistering. The foundry men sweated off pounds each and every working day – and, not surprisingly, developed a reputation as heavy drinkers.

The castings and other parts then had to be machined to the required tolerances to ensure that all the working parts fitted and worked together in perfect harmony. The specifications for engines were always very precise. A typical example is a nineteenth-century order for an engine for the SS *St Rognvald* being built in Aberdeen for the North of Scotland, Orkney and Shetland Steam Shipping Company. Every single measurement is given, in units down to $\frac{1}{8}$ of an inch, which is actually quite generous. Later specifications would be to $\frac{1}{16}$ or even $\frac{1}{32}$ of an inch. Particular attention was paid to details such as valves. The slide valves were 'to be made of hard close-grained cast-iron. These valves are to be carefully fitted to valve face by scraping, and rendered perfectly steam tight.' It is all very well demanding a steam-tight valve, but producing it was all down to the skill of the engineer.

Not every yard had its own engine shop – some simply b uilt the ship and bought the engine from an outside engineering firm. But for the big yards, this was a vital element in their success. It is not unreasonable to compare the skills of the engineers, working lathes, drills and planers with the master shipwrights of an earlier age.

The shipyards of the age of steam and iron had an immense effect on the whole community, not only on those who worked there. The noise and clamour were not kept within the works' walls, but spread out over the streets that reached right up to the yard gates. No one was unaware of the industry. The first thing many saw when they came out of their front doors in the morning was often the bows of a mighty ship rearing up, high over the rooftops. In a sense, everyone was involved in the making of ships, which was why launch days were so important to the whole community.

The arrival of new men not only changed working practices, but also had an immediate effect on the relations between workers and employers and, just as importantly in the long term, between one set of workers and another. Men had started to organise themselves in the commercial shipyards early in the eighteenth century. In the Thames yards there was a well-established method of payment. The masters provided all the materials needed on site, including heavy lifting gear such as cranes. The work was then let out to groups of men, usually between twenty and thirty, who took a contract for part of the work. If they finished ahead of time, then that was a bonus: if they were late, then they could spend the latter part of the contract working for nothing. Both sides were happy with the arrangement, but as yards grew and shipbuilding became more complex, the system began to break down. Competition for jobs grew and there were suggestions that work was going to men who had not satisfied the requirements of the guilds and had not served a full apprenticeship. The craftsmen felt that the only way they could defend their position was to band together and speak with a united voice. They needed to form a union.

The first trade unions

One of the very first was the Shipwrights Union Society, established in South Shields in 1734, but it was not a trade union in the modern sense of the word. Its main objective was to set up a society in which members could help each other out – officially known as a friendly and benevolent society. It was followed in 1795 by the South Shields Shipwrights Association, which had rather broader aims. The Combination Acts of 1799 and 1800 made virtually all trade-union activities illegal, but there were none too subtle attempts to get round the restrictions by setting up associations as mutual benefit societies, making payments to sick members and so forth. The Shipwrights Provident Union of the River Thames was formed in 1812 and it was hoped that the word 'provident' would make it seem wholly innocuous. In reality it was born out of dispute and disorder, with workers set against each other and against the masters with, in the words of the preamble to the document founding the Union, 'hypocrisy and deception making rapid inroads on the little integrity that was left'. They demanded that only those who had served the full seven-year apprenticeship should be admitted as master shipwrights, because they alone had the necessary experience to judge the quality of work being done at the yard. They also insisted that a regular system of prices for jobs should be agreed. They were quite clear on what they wanted. 'It is the intention of the members of this society, by a moral system, to support their respectability in society, and keep up the rights of their trade'. That was the problem. It is far easier to argue about and settle pay levels than it is to reach agreement on something as abstract as status. In the event, neither part of the demand was really met.

It was one thing for a union to draw up rules and regulations, but quite another to get the employers to agree to them. The London shipbuilders were unimpressed, knowing that under the Combination Acts any attempts to force them to comply would be illegal, and other employers around the country followed their example. The workers were not the only groups to form associations to protect their mutual interests. The masters also got together, and they were untouched by the Combination Acts. Events at Whitehaven in 1825 demonstrated what happened when things went badly wrong. The apprentices at Brocklebank yard found a man who was employed but who was not appropriately qualified or a member of the union. They hoisted him on a pole and marched him out into the town. There they met Mr Brocklebank, there was a scuffle and the owner was knocked over. The employers' response was immediate: no one who stayed in the union would be employed by any shipyard in the area. The men went on strike, and remained out for twenty-five weeks by which time the union's funds were exhausted and the inevitable trickle back to work began. The local paper was exultant, producing this typographical shout of triumph: 'It has let the men see the folly of ATTEMPTING TO RULE THEIR MASTERS *and made them resolve* NOT TO OFFEND SO AGAIN (!!!).'

This was only one of many bitter struggles that were to engulf the industry over the years, but the arrival of the iron ship brought a new source of discontent. Who was qualified to do what? And that was, if anything, to cause even greater problems than the disputes between men and employers. These demarcation disputes were unique to the shipping industry. We shall be seeing a lot more of them later.

Trade directories

The early part of the nineteenth century was a period of transition and change – and often quite rapid change, and not just in shipbuilding.

Improvements in printing technology meant that information that once could only be traced though hand-written documents was now far more widely available, which helps to make research a good deal easier than it is for earlier periods. New sources of information also appeared, such as directories of professionals and tradesmen within a town and city. These can make for fascinating reading. Pigot's Directory, for example, lists people in Bristol. Looking through the 1830 entries, the main connections with the sea that stand out are for masters of ships, scarcely surprising for this was still one of Britain's major ports. It is rather easy to get sidetracked by some of the stranger occupations listed – a 'printer of fancy bibles' for example or a manufacturer of orchill and cudbear. The latter turned out to be doing nothing more exotic than manufacturing dyes. In among these were six ship and boat builders. A notable absentee was Patterson's yard where Brunel's first two ships were built, but that turns up at Wapping, Bristol in the 1843 Pigot. Looking back again to 1830, you can find William Scott at the same Wapping address: a little research shows that in between the two dates, Scott went bankrupt and Patterson took over the yard. But shipbuilders are not the only names associated with the industry: there are ropemakers, sailmakers, a block and pump manufacturer and more. The directory also gives an idea of how many people had strong connections with the industry. The Acraman family at Bathurst Basin had a general iron works, but also listed specialities, making anchors, chains and boilers. William Terrell and Son of Welsh Back were even more diverse – butter and corn factors and wharfingers, but they also dressed flax and hemp, made rope, twine and sacks. By the later date, there seems to have been a big increase in activity during the previous decade with fourteen ship-builders listed. Other directories for other places can prove equally informative, and provide a very useful way to find out who exactly was building ships at that particular time. Given the names of yards, it is then possible to try and find out more about them and who they might have employed.

Newspapers

During this period, newspapers began to appear regularly. We have already seen how Whitehaven's local paper, the *Cumberland Pacquet*, took a keen if partisan interest in the local shipbuilding industry. It first appeared in 1774 and a full set of copies can be read on microfilm at the main libraries in the county. Many other shipbuilding centres also have newspapers dating back to the eighteenth century – the *Glasgow Advertiser* first appeared in 1783, the *Newcastle Courant* in 1724 and Bristol's first paper the

Bristol Post Boy came out in 1702. Not all these papers are of interest. The early Bristol papers, for example, have virtually no local news, and it is only with the appearance of *Felix Farley's Bristol Journal* in 1752 that the paper really becomes useful as a source of local information. Many of these papers can be consulted in local reference libraries, but there is also the splendid Burney Collection of eighteenth- and nineteenth-century newspapers in the British Library. Information can be obtained through the website www.bl.uk.

Early union documents

Unfortunately, information on the early days of unionism in the shipbuilding industry is scant, and the search for details is made rather more difficult by the fact that these were not national bodies, but developed at various times in different locations. A useful starting point for tracking down unions is the comprehensive list available at www.union-ancestors.co.uk. It is broken down alphabetically so that it takes some time to sort out the various shipbuilding unions from the rest. In general, it will prove more useful when looking at the latter part of the nineteenth century and beyond.

Preserved ships

As well as documentary evidence there are also a number of museums and preserved ships that help to give an insight into what the yards were producing in this period and how they worked. A number have already been mentioned in the main text. One other is of some interest. The steam launch *Dolly* was built around 1850 and still survives as part of the collection of the Windermere Steamboat Museum on the lakeside at Bowness. She is the nearest we can get to envisaging what Pettit Smith's original steam launch might have looked like. The single-cylinder engine could not be simpler, not built by some famous engineering firm, but put together by the local blacksmith. Anyone interested in seeing more of the original steam engines that first powered craft over water are well served in the Science Museum, London. Among the exhibits are Symington's original engine of 1788, a model of the *Charlotte Dundas* and the original engine from *Comet*. A replica of *Comet* can also be seen in the town centre at Port Glasgow. The Science Museum also has models showing the screw propellers of both *Francis Smith* and *Archimedes*. One other vessel deserves a special mention. HMS *Trincomalee* is the oldest British warship afloat, having been built in 1817, although she was not in fact built in Britain, but in India. She remains, however, very typical of vessels of the period and can be seen at the Historic Quay in Hartlepool.

The developments described in this chapter tell the story of the greatest upheaval to hit the world of shipbuilding for a thousand years and more. In the next chapter, we shall see how the new technology consolidated and developed, and what it meant for the workforce.

Chapter Four

THE AGE OF STEAM

*Steam power for the Royal Navy – Ironclad battleships – Naval and
private dockyards compared – Testing tanks – Steam-engine
improvements – Nineteenth-century sailing ships –
Industrial relations – Shipbuilding and union records*

Steam power for the Royal Navy

The combination of iron hull, steam engine and screw propeller set the
pattern for shipbuilding advances through the second half of the nineteenth century. The iron hull enabled ever bigger craft to be constructed.
The steam engine ultimately offered more power than sail, but more
importantly released shipping from the vagaries of the weather. The days
when ships could be becalmed for days on end or stuck in harbour, unable
to leave in the face of an adverse wind seemed numbered. The advantages
of the screw propeller are not immediately obvious and, indeed, paddle
steamers were still being constructed well into the twentieth century: the
last surviving sea-going paddle steamer in the world, the PS *Waverley*, was
built on the Clyde by A and J Inglis as recently as 1947. But she was built
to provide river excursions and short trips round the coast, not to cross the
oceans of the world. In heavy seas ships can roll extravagantly, and a
paddle steamer would be alternating between first one paddle then the
other being lifted clear of the water. The problem that exercised the minds
of engineers of the day was a simple one – which method of propulsion
was the most effective? The Admiralty were very keen to know the answer
– once they had finally got round to using steam at all.

The Navy was still relying on the wooden warships that had fought the
Napoleonic Wars throughout the early part of the nineteenth century. They
somewhat begrudgingly ordered steam tugs, which were useful for

hauling the wooden walls out of harbour until they were ready to set their sails. The first British paddle steamer to see action was not built for the Navy, but simply commandeered for use in the Burma War, that lasted from 1823–6. The *Diana* was too small to carry guns, so she was fitted with Congreve rockets, which must have looked spectacular and terrifying but inflicted little real damage.

There were two good reasons for not considering steam power for naval vessels. The first one was vulnerability. A sailing ship could suffer damage to one or more masts, lose several sails but still carry on fighting. The paddle wheel, stuck on the outside of the ship was an excellent target, and it only needed one hit to bring the engagement to an end. The other factor was the armament of the day – cannon firing broadsides. The ideal place you wanted your guns was amidships – right where the paddles were situated. The screw propeller offered a very interesting alternative, and the Admiralty put it to the test in 1845. Two identical frigates were used for the test, each fitted out with identical engines, one driving paddle wheels, the other a screw. They were fastened together, stern to stern, and the order was given to each of them to move ahead at full steam. The propeller-driven *Rattler* pulled the paddle steamer *Alecto* backwards at a speed of 4 knots. It could hardly have been a more convincing demonstration. But it still had not solved all the Admiralty's difficulties. The engine was still vulnerable. It might be thought that the iron hull would be far less of a problem than one made of wood: the opposite proved to be the case.

Cannon were giving way to rifled guns firing shells. It only needed a few experiments to convince everyone that a shell would zip straight through an iron hull, but that in doing so it would send out a lethal spray of metal fragments. Small steamers were used in the infamous Opium Wars, but as their opponents were a fleet of Chinese junks it was no contest. The Admiralty simply abandoned any attempts to modernise, and for a time gave up building warships and instead entered an agreement with the P & O line that allowed them to requisition some of their sturdy, wooden-hulled ships if needed: it was not exactly a satisfactory arrangement for the world's leading maritime power. Britannia was being asked to rule the waves in borrowed ships. Complacency would probably have continued to rule quite a lot longer, if the French had not launched a brand new warship, the *Gloire*, in 1859. She was basically a conventional wooden frigate, but what distinguished her was that the outside of the hull was hung with heavy iron plates. It was an unsophisticated answer to the problem, but she was the first armour-plated battleship. Frigates come a long way down the naval hierarchy – the name simply says that all the guns are on a single deck. But she could have demolished a whole fleet of traditional wooden walls with impunity. Something had to be done.

Ironclad battleships

The task of designing a British challenge went to Isaac Watts, Chief Constructor to the Navy, and John Scott Russell, a Scottish engineer who had worked with Brunel in constructing the SS *Great Eastern*. This new ship, the HMS *Warrior*, was to be unlike any other ship ever built. The main part of the vessel was to be, in effect, an armour-plated box with watertight bulkheads, protecting the guns and the essential machinery. It was known as the citadel. The really defining feature was the armour plating itself. Watts and Scott Russell knew that it not only had to absorb the power of a shell but also had to reduce the risk from deadly splinters. They decided to make the hull into a sandwich. The outer layer was a conventional wooden hull, with 2in thick timbers. Behind that was the main protective armour, consisting of 4½in thick wrought-iron plates. The inner layer was a backing of 18in thick teak, to absorb the last of the force of the shell and the iron fragments from impact. The protection did not extend to the bow and stern.

The steam engine was designed and built by John Penn. He had taken over his father's general engineering business at Greenwich and decided to specialise in marine steam engines. Shortly before work on *Warrior* started he had developed a new type of steam engine – the trunk engine. Earlier engines had vertical cylinders, so to convert the up and down motion of the piston to the horizontal rotating prop shaft necessitated gearing and complex arrangements, like the chain drive on the SS *Great Britain.* Penn's engine had a horizontal cylinder, with a direct drive to the crank shaft. It worked at the low pressure of 20psi, though that was considered quite high for marine engines in those days, so it needed to be massive. But the great advantage of the design was that it was very compact and the working parts were below the waterline. As the bunkers could only carry 850 tons of coal, the engines were only to be used when necessary in battle. When they were used, *Warrior* was timed on a measured mile at a speed just over 14 knots, faster than any other battleship afloat.

The rest of the time, when the engines were not in use, *Warrior* depended as her predecessors had done on sails, 48,000ft² of them on three masts. To increase efficiency under sail, the 10-ton propeller could be lifted out of the water and the two funnels could be retracted. She was a truly remarkable ship, quite unlike anything that had been built before. What is also noteworthy is how she was built. No naval dockyard could handle the job, which went instead to the Thames Iron and Shipbuilding Company at Blackwall. T J Ditchbourn, the owner, had experience in conventional wooden-ship construction, but decided that the future lay elsewhere. His yard became the first in England to be devoted entirely to the construction of iron ships. He was very much a man of the new age and, with a new partner C J Mare, began building cross Channel ferries, specifically designed to link with railway services. One has to remember that these men were developing a new technology as they went along, based rather more on trial and error than theory, and discoveries could produce unexpected consequences. In 1847, they received a dramatic proof of the strength of the iron boxes that proved the fundamental rigidity of the hull. The steamer *Prince of Wales* was launched but was left stranded, stuck at bow and stern and the retreating tide left 100ft of hull suspended in mid air. It was a disaster for the company but a boon for another engineer. Robert Stephenson was puzzling over how to build two bridges on the new Holyhead Railway, including a major span across the Menai Strait. The eventual design was an immense box girder, with the trains running inside the box – the sight of the steamer hung up unharmed had been all he needed to convince him the design would work.

So much was new about *Warrior* that it comes as something of a surprise to find that the guns were still arranged to fire broadsides, just as they had in the days of Nelson's navy. But the weapons themselves were very different. It was well known that firing shells from a gun with a rifled barrel, one with spiral thread on the inside to give the shell spin, was more accurate and that this combination had greater range than the old cannon and cannon-ball. The problem was that it was almost impossible to produce rifling on a large cast-iron gun without cracking the barrel. A solution to the problem was found by William Armstrong of Newcastle upon Tyne. As a boy he was fascinated by all things mechanical, but his father persuaded him to make a career in the law, though his old interests never left him. Invention was far more appealing than legal case work. His first major breakthrough into the world of engineering came when he invented cranes worked by hydraulic power for use at docks and harbours, and soon began manufacturing all kinds of hydraulic machinery. Original Armstrong hydraulic engines are still used, for example, to move the swing bridge across the Tyne at Newcastle. This interesting structure may seem to have very little to do with shipbuilding, but it is really quite relevant as will be explained shortly.

Armstrong now turned his attention to armaments. He began making rifled guns, and started looking for a way of constructing them with seriously large barrels. He returned to a technology that had been in use for centuries. If you take two pieces of wrought iron, bring them up to white heat and hammer them, you can weld them together to make a single piece. Armstrong took an iron bar, coiled it and hammered it to create a tube. He then welded the first tube to other tubes until he had the required length of gun barrel. This was lacking the necessary strength, so a second, slightly large tube was made and welded over the first. This required precision engineering, but the resulting barrel could easily be rifled. In 1858 a trial took place between an Armstrong 18-pounder and a conventional cast-iron gun of the same size: the new gun had half the weight of the old, fired its shell twice as far and with considerably more accuracy. It was a decisive result and *Warrior* was fitted out on her main gun deck with four 110-pounders and thirteen 68-pounders.

Armstrong set up a new armaments factory at Elswick on the Tyne above Newcastle. Naval vessels were sent up to be fitted out, so it was essential that the largest battleships would be able to reach the works. That is how it came about that when a new bridge was needed, Armstrong built the swing bridge that could be moved aside to let the ships reach his works.

Naval and private dockyards compared

A lot of space has been taken up writing about this one ship, but she has huge significance in the history of shipbuilding. The world had changed: the famous naval dockyards were still geared up for the construction of wooden walls, for attitudes were slow to change. *Warrior* was still not officially listed as a first-rate ship, though her guns could have demolished the remaining old wooden walls in one salvo. So the work was shared between a shipyard specialising in iron ships, an inventive manufacturer of steam engines and an even more inventive maker of armaments. It was also abundantly clear that the Navy would never be the same again. Once the armoured battleship had appeared nothing else could compete. The naval dockyards were forced to change. The new age needed new technologies. This was a lesson that was quickly learned by manufacturers who had no connection with the Navy and had not even in the past had anything to do with shipbuilding. One of these was a Sheffield man called John Brown.

Brown's story is one that was familiar to all those Victorians who delighted in reading the works of Samuel Smiles – the story of a man who prospered by his own native genius. Like many others in Sheffield, he was apprenticed to the metal trade after leaving school at the age of 14. And seven years later in 1837, his apprenticeship over, his father gave him a sovereign and told him he was on his own. He took over the sales side of the business that employed him, travelling around with boxes of files and cutlery. He must have been a persuasive salesman, for he soon began to think of setting up in manufacturing on his own behalf. In 1848 he invented the spring buffer for use on the railways, which he always regarded as one of his most important achievements. When in later years he was famous and publicly honoured he incorporated it into his coat of arms.

In 1850 he established the Atlas Steel and Spring Works in Sheffield. At that time steelmaking depended on importing top-grade wrought iron from Sweden. Brown made it is his main business to compete and by the 1850s the works had a dozen furnaces at work producing high-quality wrought iron. Steel could still only be made in small quantities, but that changed when Henry Bessemer invented his literally revolutionary new device for transforming pig iron into steel. Cast iron has a high carbon content and is very strong under compression, but cracks under tension. Wrought iron has virtually no carbon, is strong in tension, but crumples under compression. Steel is no more than a form of iron with carbon content part way between the other two forms, and having the virtues of both without the defects of either. The Bessemer converter was basically a giant pot mounted on trunnions. It was first tilted to be filled with molten pig iron, then returned to the vertical and air was blown through the perforated bottom, burning off the impurities. It was a sensational sight, with flames roaring out of the open top, throwing sparks in all directions.

There were a few early problems, but once these were sorted out, Brown reached an agreement with Bessemer to use his process for a payment of £1 per ton. He was still thinking mainly in terms of use on the railways and there is a delightful if not entirely reliable story of how he achieved his goal. The railway companies were reluctant to turn from their old iron rails, so late one night a gang of men were sent out from the works to the

Rolling armour plating, of the kind used on HMS Warrior *at the Atlas Steel and Spring Works in Sheffield.*

nearby Midland Railway line, levered out an iron rail and replaced it with one made of steel. In time the nearby iron rails had to be replaced: the steel one was scarcely worn.

Brown could well have continued manufacturing steel for use on the railways, but he was a man very open to new ideas. On a visit to France, he heard about the *Gloire*, which was then under construction. It was supposedly top secret but he was able to find out that the armour consisted of hammered iron plates, roughly 2ft by 5ft and 4½in thick. He was convinced that the answer was not to beat the iron into shape but to roll it. He went back to Sheffield, began experiments and eventually in 1862 he was happy enough with the results to send a sample to Portsmouth for testing against hammered plate. The trial was a huge success, and transformed his works. Where in 1857, Brown's had employed 200 men, a decade later they were employing 2,000 and turning over £1 million a year. And all the time the technology was advancing just as dramatically. In 1867, Brown's rolled the biggest armour plates the world had ever seen, an event sufficiently momentous to make it into the pages of *The Times.*

The rolling started with a slab of iron of roughly 29ft by 4ft, 21in thick and weighing 21 tons. When it had passed through the rollers several times it had been reduced to 15in thickness. Brown was full of admiration for those he called his 'brave workmen' and he had every right to be. They literally had to manhandle 20 tons of white-hot metal from the furnace and pass and repass it through the rollers in just the few minutes that were available before it became too cool to work. There were no machines involved apart from the engines driving the rollers. The work required a team of up to a hundred men working in searing temperatures. It is no wonder that publicans were keen to set up business near the factory gates so that the men could rush in at the end of the day to replace all the liquid they had sweated away.

The effect on the Navy of the new technology was equally dramatic. The Navy had been cheerfully turning out old-fashioned wooden ships of the line right up to the middle of the nineteenth century. The *Colossus* was built in 1848 at a cost of £100,000. It never saw service before it was pensioned off and sold for just over £6,000, which was no more than the value of the materials. John Brown went public in 1864, but the founder was no longer in charge when they acquired an engine and boiler works on the Clyde. They began shipbuilding, but moved from the naval to the commercial sector and in 1867 they received their first order for a screw steamer for Cunard. It was to mark the start of a partnership that was eventually to culminate in the construction of the *Queen Mary*, launched into the Clyde from the John Brown yard in 1934.

In the eighteenth century, the Navy had dominated shipbuilding, but now the positions were reversed. The naval yards were scarcely equipped to repair a ship the size of *Warrior* let alone build one, and the private sector was very happy for things to stay that way. Advances were slow at the Admiralty, partly because in the years following the Crimean War Britain was mainly at peace, so there was no great sense of urgency. Although *Warrior* was radical in so many ways, there was much that remained unchanged. Manpower was wasted on tasks that could have been simplified by the use of better designed machinery. The heavy anchors were still raised by men working a capstan as it had been in Nelson's day. Steering was made immensely difficult by the insistence of the powers that be that full helm – or the maximum movement of the rudder – should require no more than three turns. This was the rule for the old slower, smaller sailing ships, and it was obstinately clung to as an unbreakable law. No one seemed interested in the obvious fact that turning a large steamship was very different or in the notion that it could have been made easier and more efficient by the simple use of gearing. Most remarkable of all is the fact that the modern guns were still only available to be fired as broadsides through gun ports. This meant that at any one time only half the fire-power would be available in an engagement. Alternatives had already been considered and tried.

Captain Cowper Coles of the British Navy and the Swedish engineer John Ericsson had both come up with the idea of mounting guns in a rotating turret. Ericsson is an interesting man, destined it seemed at one time to be always coming second in the races to innovation. He designed a steam locomotive for use on the Liverpool & Manchester Railway, only to have his design rejected in favour of Robert Stephenson's *Rocket*. He worked on the design of a screw propeller, but Francis Pettit Smith got in first with his patent. He then left Europe for America where he turned to ship design and developed what was first called a floating battery, an ironclad warship with a turret. During the American Civil War he built the *Monitor*, a most curious vessel, where the working steam engine and crew were all beneath the waterline, with only the turret really visible on the surface. The hull was very basic, and had only a limited degree of manoeuvrability. It was rather aptly described as looking like a cheese box on a raft. On 9 March 1862 the *Monitor* engaged with the Confederate frigate *Virginia*, also officially an ironclad, but with armour that consisted of nothing more than iron rails hung outside the hull. The two unlikely vessels banged away at each other to very little effect, though it must have been a noisy nightmare for the *Monitor* crew, sealed up in their iron can. It was the first naval battle between two ironclads and the first use of a rotating turret in war.

Coles too managed to get the authorities to listen to his ideas, and the first battleship to be specifically designed for gun turrets, HMS *Devastation*, was put through trials. It was not entirely satisfactory but a second version was ordered. Although by now there was considerable experience outside the naval yards in working with iron ships, the authorities would not trust any but their own to work on this new project. The design was passed over to the inexperienced Captain Coles. The heavy superstructure resulted in a very low freeboard, so that the decks were awash even on quite a calm today. Nevertheless, HMS *Captain* was sent out for sea trials but capsized in the Atlantic, taking Coles and most of the crew with her. It was clear to many that the naval yards were simply not keeping up with the best practices elsewhere, a point forcibly made by impartial observers who took the trouble to compare working practices. One of these was P Barry, who published his report in 1863.

Barry was at once struck by the different attitudes of the employers. At Chatham he described the workforce as 'ill-paid and ill-used'. There were no facilities within the dockyard and not even a guarantee of a day's work. Men queued up at the dock gate waiting 'until the lords within thought fit to call them'. The system did not even favour the employers. To get a meal during the day and something to drink the men had to leave the yard and there was no shortage of alehouses ready to welcome them. When Barry went to Laird's at Birkenhead he found the men could get cooked meals inside the gate. His conclusion was firmly expressed, the naval dockyard workers 'cannot be expected, I will even go so far as to say, cannot be desired to labour as the artizans who are cared for, respected and encouraged not by the Messrs Laird alone, but by the other great employers of shipyard labour'.

The private employers recognised that their work called for new men with new skills. One of the key jobs was working the massive steam hammers that were now a vital part of any yard. A skilled man could operate the hammer with incredible accuracy. A famous demonstration called for putting an egg on the anvil, raising the hammer, then dropping it and bringing it to rest with the head touching the egg, but not breaking it. This may sound fanciful, but I have actually seen it done. Such men were valuable, and John Brown told Barry that he paid his hammer man £900 per annum. To which the wry comment was added: 'If then, the dockyards were to pay their hammermen £900 a year, what would we have to pay the Admiral Superintendents?' Barry left little doubt as to which he thought the more valuable.

A naval architect, Professor Edgar, was even more scathing about the inefficiencies of the naval yards. 'The traditions of the timber age have been perpetuated in the iron age. Ships are laid down in considerable numbers and a little is done now and a little done again, just as though iron became seasoned and improved after being worked into a hull.' He put it down to 'red-tapeism', an arrogance in believing that 'all the available talent of the country is employed at Whitehall' and a 'lack of business habits'. It all added up to 'a waste of money, which is little short of a public scandal'.

There was a general feeling that the Navy was not keeping up with the times, and in particular ignoring the increasingly scientific approach that was proving valuable elsewhere. The French, for example, had carried out scientific tests on stability and published the results: no one in the Admiralty considered them worth translating into English. The work of the shipwright was still considered as a craft that could be passed down through the old apprenticeship system, without any need for a theoretical basis. All this began to change with the establishment of a School of Naval Architecture at Portsmouth in 1848. The recognition of the naval architect as a professional was affirmed by the setting up of the Institute of Naval Architecture in 1860, later to become the Royal Institution of Naval Architecture. It marked the beginning of a period of change and a readiness to listen to new ideas. One of these was the development of testing ship designs by making models.

Testing tanks

There had been attempts to use models in the eighteenth century, when different rigs were tested out on a pond, but the real breakthrough was down to a man who had begun his career as a railway engineer. William Froude had worked with Brunel on the Great Western Railway and his first introduction to ships came when he was asked to advise on the launch of the *Great Eastern*. This was an event that went catastrophically wrong, very largely because no one had ever tried to launch a ship of that size before, and the arrangements for launching would only be tested on the day itself. The launch was set for 3 November 1857, but was not only a complete failure but cost the life of one of the workmen. The ship was finally floated on 30 January the following year. It has never been recorded, but it could be that Froude began even then to think that testing new ideas on a full-sized ship was not necessarily the best way of going about things. Only one life had been lost in the launch, but the sinking of Coles' experimental HMS *Captain* was clearly down to poor design, which was only discovered too late to save the ship and the men aboard. Froude put his ideas to the Institute of Naval Architects, who approved them and with their backing he approached the Admiralty. He knew that anything that smacked of criticism of their methods would be fatal to his scheme, so he took a very different approach: model testing could save money. Improved design could result in a big saving in material costs in construction and running costs in service. The Admiralty approved and paid £2,000 towards building

A modern model being tested at the Denny Tank in Dumbarton.

a tank at Torquay. The tests showed conclusively that work done with models gave an accurate indication of what would happen with a real ship at sea. The private sector was not slow to build on this initiative, and soon the first commercial tank was under construction.

William Denny was a Clydeside shipbuilder who showed that he was open to new ideas. He was the first to institute speed tests on a measured mile for every craft that left the yard, and encouraged all the workers to suggest improvements in yard practices through an incentive scheme. He at once saw the advantages of using models and built a tank by his works at Dumbarton. Begun in 1881, it remained in commercial use for a century. The tank itself is 300ft long and 8ft deep. A mechanical device is used to agitate the water to create waves of different heights and the model ships are towed along by a carriage moving above the water. The models themselves are made out of wax, which allows for easy modification: it is no more difficult to add more wax than it is to trim some away. There is a splendid nineteenth-century machine for transforming the naval architect's drawings into a three-dimensional hull shape. The operator follows the contours on the plan, which are then replicated in the cutting tool. The last big ship to be tested here was the P & O liner *Canberra* launched in 1960 – a remarkable testament to the value of Froude's inspiration. The Denny Tank is currently both a museum and a working research facility.

Steam-engine improvements

In the naval establishment's slow move towards modernity the generally accepted view is that the new men were being held back by the establishment, yet in one area at least it was a naval officer of impeccably aristocratic pedigree who was a practical advocate for change. Thomas Cochrane, Tenth Earl of Dundonald had a highly successful naval career as a serving officer, though one not untouched by scandal, and a considerably less successful time in politics. Near the end of his life he took an interest in the new technology. In the 1840s he became an advocate of steam power and designed a new type of boiler that was fitted into HMS *Janus* in 1844. The first steam boilers had been little more than large iron vessels heated by external fires, like overgrown kettles sat on hobs. The boiler on the pioneering paddle steamer *Charlotte Dundas* had been built in just this way, with the firebox held in place by brickwork. It was probably the first and last time that bricklayers had taken an active role in shipbuilding. Cochrane's boiler was very different. The furnaces were an integral part of the boiler. There were three of them opening into a common combustion chamber. This was a decided improvement, but was still not able to produce steam at a greater pressure than about 30psi. A far better system was later adopted based on innovations in the world of railways.

There was no great rush to increase boiler pressure, largely because of fears for what would happen if anything went wrong. And things did go wrong. On the first voyage of Brunel's *Great Eastern* a mistake by one of the ship's engineers resulted in two cocks being closed that should have been open, and as a result pressure built until there was an almighty explosion. The deck planks above the boiler were shattered and one of the funnels was blown high in the air. Throughout the history of the development of high-pressure steam it was all too often the case of human error: too many were in charge of engines who did not fully realise the dangers. Stories from the railways of drivers trying to keep on schedule by fastening down the safety valve to get extra steam were widespread: and the numbers of accidents involving boiler explosions suggest that they may not have been exaggerated. The shipbuilders needed to be extra cautious. A boiler explosion in a factory might kill the engineman; the footplate crew on a locomotive might end up dead or injured. These were tragedies. But an explosion on a ship could sink an entire vessel with passengers and crew. But by the middle of the nineteenth century, improved technology and greater expertise were combining to improve safety. It was time for those changes to be shown in ships, and the way forward had already been demonstrated on the railways in 1829.

One of the most important elements in Robert Stephenson's innovative locomotive *Rocket* was the multi-tubular boiler. In this the hot gases from the firebox passed through the water down a series of tubes. A similar system was eventually developed for use in ships with the Scotch boiler, first introduced in 1862. Now far higher pressures were available and the next important question was how to use it efficiently. The main advantage of high pressure is that you can get as much power from an engine with a small cylinder as you can from a big engine working at low pressure. That is not the end of the story, however. In practice, not all the steam pressure could be turned into useful work: the exhaust steam was still under pressure. The answer was to add a second cylinder alongside the first. Steam from the high-pressure cylinder instead of disappearing up the funnel, now passed straight into the second low-pressure cylinder. In order to get the same power output from them both the low-pressure cylinder had to be made bigger than the high pressure. A further refinement was to condense the exhaust steam, which provided a supply of feed water for the boiler. Before that sea water had been used with several unfortunate consequences. The whole system was taken a step further with the three-cylinder, triple-expansion engine. The first of these engines was installed by John Elder of Glasgow in the *Propontis* in 1864. It was not an immediate success, simply because boiler construction had not yet advanced sufficiently to its needs. A year later a second trial with a new steam boiler producing steam at 125psi was a triumph. Three elements had come together: a new type of engine, an improved boiler and an appropriate material – steel. The greater efficiency offered by this system meant that shipbuilders were able to build bigger and faster vessels than ever before. It seemed as if the age of sail had finally come to an end, but in fact it still had many years to go.

Nineteenth-century sailing ships

However efficient the new engines might be, a steamer could only go on very long voyages by stopping to refuel somewhere along the way. In the first decades of the nineteenth century, ships bound for the Far East had to take the long route round the tip of Africa. Coaling stations were virtually non-existent so the only alternative was sail. A very special trade developed in the nineteenth century. There was a huge demand for China tea

An illustration from a nineteenth-century steam-engine text book showing a typical marine compound engine.

and immense premiums were paid for the first of the new season's crop. The sailing ships of the day raced to grab that bonus, and designers tried to make their ships faster than those of the rivals. The clipper ship was developed in America, characterised by a long, narrow hull and steeply raked hollow bows. Americans could well have dominated the trade but for the outbreak of Civil War in the 1860s. British shipbuilders seized their chance. In 1869 the Scott and Linton yard at Dumbarton built a new clipper. Being a good Scots firm, they looked for a name in the writings of the national poet, Robert Burns. They settled on the story of Tam o'Shanter, who was pursued by a witch wearing a short shrift or cutty sark. The figurehead shows the scantily clad witch clutching a bunch of hairs from Tam's horse's tail.

The *Cutty Sark* had scarcely entered service before the Suez Canal opened and steamers took over the route. That left just one lucrative trade –

A typical nineteenth-century shipyard, with both sailing ships and steamers being built side by side. This is the Barclay Curle yard on the Clyde in 1845.

bringing wool from Australia. Up to 5,000 bales of wool were stacked in the hold. There was precious little space left for the crew, who had meagre accommodation. The ship could carry up to thirty-four sails, which added up to about three-quarters of an acre of canvas. And all this had to be managed by a crew of just nineteen, working day and night in watches. Yet on her best run she covered the distance from Sydney to London in just sixty-seven days. This was a remarkable achievement and this famous ship continued trading under sail right through to 1922. She was given a permanent home at Greenwich, but suffered severe damage from a fire in 2007.

Even yards such as Lairds of Birkenhead, which specialised in steamers, were still building sailing ships until late in the nineteenth century, as were other yards. And in some of these the new technology of the age spilled over into the traditional world of the sailing ship. Robert Thompson & Sons of Sunderland built forty-two sailing ships, mostly barques, between 1865 and 1892. What distinguished them from older vessels was their construction: hull, masts and spars were all made out of iron and steel. One of these, the *Lady Elizabeth*, came to grief and ended her days as a wreck in the Falkland Islands. She is still there, lying in shallow water, with a large hole in the hull, but with her three metal masts still standing. Not everyone was

A close up of one of the riveted iron masts on the Lady Elizabeth, *a Sunderland-built vessel, now a wreck in the Falkland Islands.*

impressed by the use of iron in sailing ships. Alexander Stephen reverted to wooden planking for the hull, simply because it was less prone to fouling than iron.

The big yards are well known, but throughout Britain in the nineteenth century there were large numbers of vessels being built for the coastal trade and even for transoceanic voyages. The development of industries in Wales, for example, brought a new demand for ships. On Anglesey, the discovery of huge deposits of copper at Parys Mountain resulted in the establishment of a new port at Amlwch. Here Captain William Thompson set up a boat yard, specialising in the construction of schooners and barquentines, and his son continued in the business, constructing in iron and steel, long after the copper trade had ended. The remains of the dry dock where the vessels were built can still be seen. The development of the slate trade in North Wales was an even more powerful incentive for ship-building. The creation of a new harbour at Porthmadog in the 1820s soon resulted in a major shipbuilding enterprise, begun by Henry Jones. The demand grew as a busy slate trade developed between Wales and Germany, as a result of which 146 vessels were built at Porthmadog between 1848 and 1878. The last schooners to be built at the port were

A billhead showing Captain William Thomas's yard at Amlwch on Anglesey in 1880.

generally recognised as some of the most beautiful sailing ships ever built and became known as the 'Western Ocean Yachts'.

The two worlds of sail and steam co-existed throughout the nineteenth century, as did the different traditions involved in building them. What is notable about the pioneers of steamship development is that very often the experience they built on was gained outside the shipbuilding industry. James Howden was born in Scotland in 1832 and became an engineering apprentice at the age of 15. He began working for a manufacturer specialising in steam engines for use in foundries. It was soon obvious that he had exceptional abilities and even before his apprenticeship was over he was appointed chief draughtsman. By the age of 22 he had set up as an independent engineering consultant, and was soon turning his attention to the design of marine boilers. His first two designs were for multi-tubular boilers delivering steam at what was then the exceptional pressure of 100psi. He bought up an old engineering works in Glasgow and founded Howden Engineering. He was still under 30. He was as far removed from the traditional shipwright as could be imagined, constantly experimenting with new technologies. His most successful innovation was the introduction of 'forced draught', which used a fan to blow hot air through the fire. This was an idea that had its origins in his earlier work with foundry engines – hot blast for iron furnaces had been introduced in the 1830s to increase furnace temperatures. The Howden system was given a trial in the *City of New York* on a voyage from Scotland to Trinidad in 1884. There was a small increase in power, but a huge saving in fuel consumption, using just two-thirds of the coal that was normally burned. The result was so dramatic that by the end of the century a thousand steamships had been fitted with the Howden System of Forced Draught. Howden was equally innovative at his own works site. New buildings were added, and the construction was broken down into a series of stages, in a simple form of assembly line.

Industrial relations

New attitudes also appeared in the relationship between some masters and their employees. Patronage had been common in the yards, and 'premium apprentices' were young men whose parents had paid for their positions, and they were often the sons of ship owners or other shipbuilders. These privileged youngsters were also referred to as 'gentlemen apprentices', though William Denny had another name for them– 'petted darling'. In his view the premium apprentice never made good – 'he is a child wrapped in cotton wool'. Denny believed that the only things that deserved reward were hard work and initiative. This was a view shared by James Napier who introduced a profit-sharing system for his workers as early as 1850 at his Govan yard. It was all based on a scale system, where 'labourers or helpers & boys' got a smaller proportion than the charge hands. He was, however, quite stern: 'I have entirely excluded those who unfitted them-selves for their duty by their drinking habits'. This was a time before licensing hours were introduced, and men did not have to wait for the end of the working day to get a drink – they could stop off on their way in. And quite a few did.

The nineteenth century saw a revolution in shipbuilding. The naval dock-yards that had dominated the industry for so long shrank in importance for a time while the private yards developed. An industry that had depended for centuries on slow changes introduced by generations of craftsmen working within an established tradition was all but overwhelmed by new men, working with new ideas that came from the very different world of engineering. Shipbuilding had become altogether more complex. The ship-wright no longer wandered off to the forest to select his timber and then left it to mature at the yard ready for work to start. Now the iron or steel plates were ordered from foundries and forges in great industrial centres such as Sheffield. The hull might be constructed in the shipyard, but essen-tials such as the engine and the boiler might be made quite independently. Perhaps the most important change of all was the need for the industry to find a new, far bigger workforce, equipped with very different skills, and skills that owed little or nothing to the 'mysteries' of the ancient crafts of the shipwrights.

Shipbuilding and union records

Looking for ancestors in the nineteenth-century world of shipbuilding now involves searching for different kinds of occupations. The old names still existed but new ones were added to the list – platers, riveters, machinists and engineers joined the ranks of shipwrights, caulkers and riggers. There was also what many regarded as an even more startling change. Women and girls were employed for the first time, for example as tracers in drawing offices. The other noticeable change came in the way in which work was distributed. In the eighteenth century, activity had been mainly concentrated in the south. By the 1870s three-quarters of the workforce was employed north of the line from Bristol to London. The greatest change of all came on the Clyde where the manufacture of steamships had begun and where it developed most rapidly. At this time Clydeside yards were employing about 25,000 men, nearly half the workforce building iron ships in Britain. The rest of the work was divided up, with the north-east of England being the next most important region, the Thames coming a very poor third and the north-west making a substantial contribution. It is inevitably in the north that the greatest number of family connections will be found for this period. This does not necessarily mean that the workforce originated in these areas. The rapidly developing industry was desperate to find workers with the appropriate skills. For many families, this is the point where the first connection with the industry was made. Before that many would have worked in other branches of the engineering or iron industries.

A new, complicating factor now appears in the story. If one looks to Scotland and the Clyde, for example, there were over twenty yards at work by the 1860s. It is difficult to tell from sources such as census returns exactly which yard a man was employed in. On the other hand the nature of the work is easier to determine: it is quite usual to find even a general labourer being listed quite specifically as 'shipyard labourer'. But it was not just the yards that were intimately involved in the industry. In many cases the engines, the boilers, copper and brass fittings, even upholstery would come from Glasgow itself. It is perfectly logical to argue that the man who makes the engine for a ship is every bit as much a shipbuilder as the one who erects the hull. A few of these general engineering firms later established a leading role in shipbuilding, even when they started in quite different directions. Charles Randolph set up in business in Glasgow as a millwright, making machinery of all kinds for everyone from textile manu-facturers to gunpowder makers. It was not until 1852 that he began making marine steam engines, and soon this came to dominate his business. He took a partner and as Randolph & Elder they were to play a leading role in the development of the steam engine. Later still, they expanded into the construction of iron ships as well as engines. They, at least, will show up in shipbuilding references. Other concerns, such as Parkhead forge, were wholly owned by shipbuilders, a fact that is not immediately obvious when the name comes up in the records.

Union records become a more important source of information towards the latter part of the nineteenth century. The Society of Friendly Boilermakers was founded in 1834, but changed its name to the United Friendly Boilermakers Society and in 1852 changed again to the United Society of Boilermakers and Iron and Steel Shipbuilders, by which time they appeared to be happy that everyone was included. The shipwrights' unions were gradually losing ground, and they were handicapped by being divided between a host of local unions. In 1882 the process of amal-gamation got under way with the formation of the Associated Society of Shipwrights made up of eighteen small unions: others were to join later.

Many of the documents for individual unions are spread around various archives, centred on the main shipbuilding centres, but a useful starting place is the Working Class Movement Library, which has a special section designed to help research into family history. They are based in Salford and details can be found at www.wcml.org.uk.

The nineteenth century was a period that saw a huge expansion in the number of yards, particularly in the construction of iron steamships, and company archives now become much more important. Unfortunately not all records have survived, and those for the smaller yards can rarely be found. That does not mean that no information is available. Take the case of the Porthmadog vessels mentioned earlier. If, from census returns or other documents, you locate an ancestor employed in the industry in that area during the second half of the nineteenth century, then he would almost certainly have been employed by either David Jones or David Williams. A great deal is known about these two keen rivals and a lot of information can be found in the county archives. The same is true of many areas around the coast of Britain. Most of these small concerns, however, were involved in making sailing vessels, from fishing smacks to fully rigged ships. They could never master the capital or the resources to enter the world of steel and steam.

Chapter Five

A GOLDEN AGE

*Warships – Steam turbines and ocean liners – Blue Riband of the
Atlantic – Foreign competition – Industrial disputes – Small yards and
local archives – Company and union records*

Warships

The second half of the nineteenth century marked a period in British ship-building history, which was as notable for innovation as it was for increased output. It is interesting to look at two developments that were down to the personal initiative of two men from very different backgrounds.

Alfred Fernandez Yarrow was born in London in 1842. His father was a merchant, who also saw himself as a successful and shrewd entrepreneur, a belief that unfortunately cost the family their wealth. Invited to invest in a copper mine he was at least sensible enough to ask for an ore sample for assay. When the results came back they were more than encouraging: it was ore of the very highest quality, so he put all his spare money into the enterprise. Sadly he had forgotten to make sure of one important fact: whether or not the ore actually came from the mine he was asked to support! The money was lost, and young Alfred's schooling ended at the age of 15, when he was apprenticed to a firm of marine engineers. In the event it probably did him a favour, for he was a young man who delighted in mechanical devices and invention. His earliest recorded invention was a candle snuffer for his grandmother. As soon as her head hit the pillow, it jerked a string and the light went out.

As an apprentice he made friends with James Hilditch and they rigged up an electric telegraph between their homes. Together they made a number of inventions that they patented, including a steam plough and a novel

Steam launches at the Yarrow yard on the Thames.

kind of steam carriage, neither of which was particularly successful. However, they made enough money to set up in business for themselves as general engineers. They settled on a site on the Thames at the Isle of Dogs, hoping to specialise in boat repair. Yarrow was still only 23 years old. He rowed up and down the river touting for work, but they only got jobs by severe price cutting, with the result that the more jobs they got the more money they lost. Having spent £1,000 setting up the yard, by the end of the first year they had recorded losses of £2,000. It must have seemed that young Yarrow had inherited his business sense from his father, whatever inventive genius he may have had. In a last attempt to salvage the venture they set up a new business, making steam launches. Having got one order – which again failed to make a profit – he took a picture of the handsome vessel, had it copied and stuck up posters in pubs and inns up and down the Thames. The advertising campaign worked. Between 1868 and 1875 they built 150 launches, before the partnership was dissolved. Yarrow was ready to move on to other things.

Yarrow devised a system for making iron launches in sections that could be used for exploration. The parts could be carried overland then assembled on site. The most famous example was *Le Stanley*, built for the explorer H M Stanley. It came in nine sections, each of which could be fitted with wheels for use as a cart until water was reached, when the parts could be bolted together to make a boat. But his real breakthrough that turned Yarrow's into one of the more important yards in Britain came with the development of a new weapon. During the American Civil War Confederate Captain Hunter Davidson designed the spar torpedo. It consisted of an explosive charge mounted on the end of a long spar. This was fastened to a rowing boat, which would charge at the target, rather like a waterborne knight at a joust, and would then be rowed backwards as fast as the sailors could manage. It was difficult to see who was most likely to suffer: attacked or attacker. Yarrow had the idea that a steam launch might have more chance of getting away after the explosion than a rowing boat, but before he could develop his plans, a new version of the torpedo was invented. This was a self-propelled device, which could be released while still some distance from the target. Yarrow at once saw that the fast launch would be the ideal torpedo boat.

At first the British Admiralty showed little interest, and the initial orders came from Japan and Russia. Eventually the Admiralty agreed to take a few vessels, but they quibbled about the price and made stipulations. They demanded a speed of 18 knots and an agreed amount was to be knocked off the price for every knot that the vessel fell below that figure. Yarrow consented, but only on condition that the same amount should be added for every extra knot obtained. The Admiralty were convinced they would be the winners, but Yarrow had been making his own experiments. Propeller design had never been scientifically investigated, and designers took the seemingly logical step of making bigger blades to obtain more speed. Yarrow tried the opposite and it worked: at the trials his torpedo boats were recorded at just under 30 knots.

Each new step forward in warfare technology creates a demand for another development to counteract it. Yarrow set out to build sleek, fast warships capable of overtaking and outgunning the torpedo boats. In designing them he had to introduce a new type of boiler able to withstand very high pressures. If the torpedo boat had its origins in luxury launches pottering up the Thames on a sunny, Sunday afternoon, the new boiler had an even less likely origin. The inspiration came from the bicycle. A new technique had been developed for making bicycle frames by drawing out steel tubes instead of welding them, and this was what Yarrow used for his boilers. The first two vessels, 180ft long by just 18ft beam were launched in 1892 and reached speeds of over 27 knots. They were given a brand new name – destroyers. By now Yarrow had become aware that shipbuilding on the Thames was coming to an end. At the beginning of the twentieth century he moved operations to the Clyde. What is remarkable about this story is not just the progress from launch to destroyer, but that little more than thirty years had passed since the launch of *Warrior*, a vessel that for all her innovations still looked back to days when naval battles would be fought as they had been in Nelson's day.

Steam turbines and ocean liners

Charles Parsons' early life was very different from that of Yarrow. He was the youngest son of the Third Earl of Rosse. He was brought up in Ireland where he was privately educated, but, unusually for the time, his tutors put a high priority on science. He went on to Trinity College Dublin followed by two years at Cambridge, during which time he studied pure and applied mathematics. The universities offered no practical engineering training so he went for an apprenticeship to Armstrong's at Elswick, followed by two years at Kitson's in Leeds. He developed a new kind of steam engine and became interested in torpedoes. By 1884 he had acquired sufficient experience and shown enough initiative to be offered a junior partnership at Clarke, Chapman & Co. at Gateshead.

This was an exciting time for a new technology: the generation of electricity. In 1882 the very first electric power station had been opened in London for street lighting, and the Gateshead company was among the first to start manufacturing generators. The use of conventional steam engines with the drive taken by belts from the flywheels meant that the maximum speed possible was no more than 1,500 revolutions per minute (rpm). Parsons was put in charge of the new electricity department and at once began working on an engine in which the steam instead of making a piston go up and down would rotate blades in the cylinder. It would be a steam turbine. By 1884 he had produced his first turbo-dynamo, working at 18,000rpm. It was an immediate success. At the same time he took out a patent for a steam turbine to power a ship. It was not until 1893, however, that he began serious experiments. By 1894 he had set up his own marine turbine company on the Tyne at Wallsend.

There were a number of problems to be overcome, not least how to find an appropriate propeller design to convert the fast shaft speed into speed over the water. After a number of experiments, involving tests on a pond using models powered by rubber bands, he designed a full-scale test vessel, officially described as a yacht, *Turbinia*. First results were disappointing, and he suspected that the single propeller was causing voids in the water. Science was brought in, with a test tank, strobe lighting and a camera to capture the effect of the propeller. The result confirmed Parsons' theory and the result was a major redesign with multiple propellers. The results were astonishing: speed rose from a very modest

20 knots to 34 knots, a far higher speed than any other vessel afloat. There is a popular story about the great naval review at Spithead in 1897. The pride of the British Navy was drawn up on display, when this funny little craft came dashing across the front of them. An infuriated Admiral ordered it apprehended, but no craft could catch it. Sadly the story is untrue: *Turbinia* had been officially invited, but even so her speed astonished the watchers.

Turbinia would never have made much of a yacht. She was built for speed with no thought for comfort. At 100ft long and 9ft beam she was more like a missile than a conventional craft. The engine room is almost filled with machinery and the stokers must have been very short: I found when I was filming on board some years ago that I could not even stand upright in the engine room. Everything was sacrificed to speed. She can now be seen on display at the Discovery Museum at Newcastle upon Tyne.

It was not only the Navy that needed speed. One of the greatest challenges facing ship owners was to have the fastest vessels, especially on the highly profitable Atlantic routes between Europe and North America. Today we look back on these crossings through the gauze of nostalgia, perhaps thinking of the voyages as being not unlike taking a trip on a

Parsons' experimental steam yacht Turbinia, *now preserved in the Discovery Museum at Newcastle upon Tyne.*

modern luxury cruise ship. Many of the great liners were indeed luxurious, but there the similarity ends. Cruise ships call in at interesting places: on a liner the ocean you see when you go to bed looks exactly the same as the one you see when you get up. Cruises generally favour placid seas: the North Atlantic is seldom placid. Why is speed important? For exactly the same reason that a ship's designer gave when he was asked why he made the saloons and other public rooms resemble gentlemen's clubs or the lounges of first-class hotels instead of giving them a suitably nautical air: because the last thing most passengers want is to be reminded that they are at sea at all. Charles Dickens crossed to America on a paddle steamer in January 1842 and no one would ever use his account to advertise the delights of a sea voyage.

> But what the agitation of a steam-vessel is, on a bad winter's night in the wild Atlantic, it is impossible for the most vivid imagination to conceive. To say that she is flung down on her side in the waves, with her masts dipping into them, and that, springing up again, she rolls over on the other side, until a heavy sea strikes her with the noise of a hundred great guns, and hurls her back – that she stops, and staggers, and shivers, as though stunned, and then, with a violent throbbing at her heart, darts onward like a monster goaded into madness, to be beaten down, and battered, and crushed, and leaped on by the angry sea – that thunder, lightning, hail, and rain, and wind, are all in fierce contention for the mastery – that every plank has its groan, every nail its shriek, and every drop of water in the great ocean its howling voice – is nothing.

In other words, the sooner the passenger is released from this misery the better for all but the most enthusiastic sailors. The faster the ship, the more popular it was likely to be, and all the great shipbuilders vied with each other to create vessels that would break the transatlantic record. It was not just a matter of prestige: it was a question of profit as well. The faster the crossing, the more crossings you could make in a year. The largest ships of the period might have 20,000 passengers, so even a single extra trip meant another 20,000 tickets sold. And the shipbuilders of Britain were no longer looking just at a home market. They were now looking to make ships for the world. The story of this period is largely one of the struggle to make ships bigger and faster than ever before.

Blue Riband of the Atlantic

One man who was especially associated with the search for more speed is William Pearce. His background was the very conventional one of training as a shipwright and naval architect at Chatham, where he soon made a reputation for himself. In 1861 he was put in charge of the construction of HMS *Achilles*, the first ironclad to be built at a naval yard. But three years later he had left to take over at Robert Napier's yard on the Clyde. This was an exciting time. A C Kirk had just developed the triple-expansion engine here and Pearce wanted to make the most of it. He suggested that there should be a competition, open to all nations, to see which ships could make the fastest transatlantic crossings, with the winner being awarded what became known as the Blue Riband of the Atlantic. Pearce at once got the yard busy preparing to build a ship to claim the prize, the *Arizona*. In 1879 she made the fastest crossing with a time of 7 days, 10 hours and 53 minutes. Napier vessels were to repeat the victory seven times between then and 1893, when the *Campania* took 5 days, 14 hours and 24 minutes. Pearce himself had died in 1888, his dream of the 'five-day ship' still unrealised. But what he had done was oversee the transformation of the shipyard into a major industrial concern. The site at Govan covered 70 acres and employed around 5,000 men. The changes and developments

Steam hammers at the Linthouse engine works of Alexander Stephen & Son.

in technology were calling for any shipyard that hoped to compete on the world stage not just to grow in size but also to develop more sophisticated ways of working than had been seen in the past.

One of the companies that rose to the challenge was Alexander Stephen & Son. They decided that the time had arrived to expand and modernise and in 1869 they bought a site at Linthouse to the west of Govan. Here they set out a new works, incorporating the latest ideas in technology. The most impressive building was the Engine House, designed to contain all the heavy machinery for constructing ships' engines in the one workshop. To keep as much space as possible free, the whole structure was constructed on a cast-iron frame, and was open to the roof, where skylights provided good, overall illumination. When work finally came to an end in the late twentieth century the whole structure was dismantled and re-erected at the Scottish Maritime Museum at Irvine. The giant steam hammers that were once the main features have gone, but there are still a number of impressive machine tools, which help to give an idea of what the workshop would have been like a hundred years ago.

It was not simply a case of established yards developing to meet the new demands: new men were coming into the industry from different backgrounds and bringing new ideas. Edward Harland was the son of a Yorkshire doctor, who was a close friend of the great railway engineer George Stephenson. As a result, Edward was apprenticed in 1846 to what was then one of the leading manufacturers of steam locomotives in the world, Robert Stephenson of Newcastle upon Tyne. Family connections proved equally useful when his apprenticeship ended. An uncle introduced him to Gustav Schwabe, a German financier who was a major investor in the Liverpool shipping line John Bibby & Sons. Schwabe used his influence to get Harland a job at a shipyard on the Clyde where Bibby ships were being built. He moved on from there to the Tyne and in 1854 took the post as general manager to Robert Hickson's shipyard in Belfast. Harland proved himself to be one of those rare individuals who combined engineering abilities with stern financial discipline. Under his strict control the yard survived a severe slump in its fortunes and Harland was able to return family favours: he appointed Schwabe's nephew, Gustav Wolff, as his assistant. Whether it was entirely down to the merits of the new yard or a simple extension of the nepotism that seems to run through this story, Harland at once received an order to build three ships for Bibby.

Harland then showed that he was his own man. He made radical changes to the ships' designs. The vessels were given steel decks to increase rigidity, and in place of the usual rounded hull, they were built with very flat bottoms and straight sides, which increased their capacity. Their unusual shape led to them being known as 'Bibby's coffins'. But the company was

A massive boiler leaving the Harland and Wolff yard in Belfast.

well pleased with them, and more orders followed. Harland took Wolff on as a partner and the famous company was born in 1861. Harland had received his initial training in the works of the man who had given the world the first modern steam locomotive, *Rocket*, and had stayed in business by pursuing innovation and remaining at the forefront of design. He and Wolff were to follow the same path. They invested in all the latest machinery, established their own engine works, and as soon as it became clear that steel from a new process, the open hearth, was becoming available they had the yard adapted to make use of it. It was this progressive approach that led to a connection with Thomas Ismay, and earned them contracts to build for his White Star line. In 1898 the *Engineer* contained an article deploring the state of much of British industry, which was slow to modernise machinery and working methods, but exonerated the shipbuilding industry:

> They may fairly claim to be the leaders of the world in the development of new systems of ship-building and to be the most open-handed of all nations in the trial of elaborate and costly experiments, and in the construction of expensive tools and apparatus. Of all our great firms there is probably not one which watches more

*The battleship
Blanco Encalada
ready to be
launched from
Armstrong's at
Elswick in 1894.
She was built for
the Chilean navy.*

closely the modern development of machinery and the applications
of it to their own craft than Messrs. Harland and Wolff.

The machine tools in use in the yard were impressive: machines for
punching holes that could go through 1½in-thick steel plate and others that
could plane plates up to 30ft long, as well as the drills and lathes that might
be found in any engineering works. And they were all British made,
coming from manufacturers in Manchester and Glasgow. Harland had
been among the first to appreciate the importance that steel would have in
the industry, and the steel manufacturers themselves were no less astute.
In 1903 the Sheffield steel company Charles Cammell & Co. Ltd took over
the Laird yard on the Mersey to form Cammell Laird. They soon established an association with Fairfield and John Brown to create a consortium

specifically designed to sell naval ships to foreign governments. It was this combination of modernisation that gave British shipbuilding its edge and helped it maintain its position in the face of increasing foreign competition. The challenge was becoming increasingly serious.

Foreign competition

At the end of the nineteenth century German shipyards began a move to bigger ships with more powerful engines. In place of the triple-expansion engine they brought in the quadruple-expansion. This development culminated in the *Kaiser Wilhelm II* of 1903, which actually had two sets of these engines driving twin propeller shafts. At 25,000 tons, she was 700ft long and had a top speed of over 23 knots. She was built for the Norddeutscher Lloyd Company and was undoubtedly the finest passenger liner of her day, intended for the prestigious North Atlantic trade. With a full crew and passenger list she carried 2,500 people on board. There was another requirement, insisted on by the German Admiralty: she had to be built in such a way that in wartime she could have guns fitted and serve as a cruiser. Ironically, she did have a wartime role, but not quite what was intended. Captured by the Americans, she was transformed into a troopship and renamed *Agamemnon* in 1917. But the significance of this potential battleship was not lost on the British Admiralty. Britain needed ships that would be even bigger and faster than *Kaiser Wilhelm II*: the Blue Riband would have to be won back.

An agreement was reached with Cunard to build two liners, and it was a very good bargain for the line. They received a low-interest loan of £2.6 million and an annual subsidy of £150,000 for running costs. The requirements were simply expressed. The two ships must be capable of maintaining an average speed of 24–25 knots across the Atlantic in normal conditions. Two yards were initially chosen for the work, but as the design progressed so the proposed size of the ships kept increasing. One of the proposed yards, Vickers & Maxim of Barrow, had to drop out: they were simply too small at that time and could not cope. So it was decided that one of the pair, the *Mauretania*, would be built at Swan Hunter on the Tyne and the other, the *Lusitania*, at John Brown on the Clyde.

The construction of these two ships epitomised the very best practices of the day. It was no longer enough for the shipbuilders to decide for themselves on the standards of safety they would set. Regulations demanded that a ship should be able to cope with encountering a wave with a wavelength equal to the length of the ship and a height, measured from trough to peak, equal to 5 per cent of the length. In the case of these vessels that meant they had to withstand the impact of a 35ft high wave. The stresses had to be measured against the extreme conditions. In a trough there would be a tendency to sag as waves try to lift bow and stern, while at a peak there would be the opposite effect, hogging, with a tendency for the bow and stern to droop. To overcome both problems it was decided to reinforce the midships area with high tensile steel. All these factors had to be examined before work began, which involved model tests in a tank and trials using a powered launch. This process lasted for two years, and in the meantime the yards were preparing for the work ahead.

At Swan Hunter a new covered shed was built, an immense structure 150ft high with a 100ft-span glass roof and fitted out with seven overhead electric cranes. All the latest technology was incorporated. In place of the iron rivets heated in a brazier, the rivets were now made of mild steel heated in electric furnaces. There were to be 400 million of them, set in place using the new hydraulic riveters instead of the old-fashioned hammers. The machinery was on a scale never attempted before. Where the German ship had relied on piston engines, these vessels had the latest Parsons turbines: four for forward drive and two for reverse. These were not the only Parsons engines on board. There were also four electric generators, providing enough power to run a small town. The ships certainly had a large population. They were designed to hold 560 first-class passengers, 475 in second class and 1,300 in third class. The passengers would have been aware of the 376 members of the purser's staff who looked after them and the 70 sailors they saw working the ship. What they did not see was the so-called 'black gang' – 366 men below decks in the engine rooms.

Swan Hunter had everything close at hand, but Brown's had to order larger castings from Sheffield. They were brought by traction engines, which frequently broke down trying to cross over Shap Fell in Cumberland, though as a manager at the yard noticed, it always seemed to happen rather close to the front door of the Shap Inn.

As Swan Hunter prepared for the launch they had to dredge the river opposite the yard to take such an immense vessel. Both of the new ships entered service in 1907 and the *Mauretania* proved slightly the faster of the two. That year she established a new eastbound Atlantic record, completing the crossing at an average speed of 24 knots and held onto the record for twenty-two years, an extraordinary achievement. Cunard's greatest rival was Ismay's White Star line, and he too commissioned two new liners to be built at Harland and Wolff. They too had innovative features, including watertight bulkheads that could be operated electrically from the bridge in the event of an accident. One of the pair, *Olympic*, enjoyed a successful career, finally being sent to the breaker's yard after twenty-three years in service. Her sister ship was less fortunate: she was, of course, the *Titanic*. The *Lusitania* was also to suffer a disaster, sunk by a German U-boat in the First World War.

The research that had led to the completion of the *Mauretania* and *Lusitania* was very promptly used by the Admiralty to create an entirely new type of battleship. HMS *Dreadnought* was built at Portsmouth, and, like the two liners, was fitted out with Parsons turbines, giving her a top speed of 21 knots. Her main armament consisted of five turrets, each housing two 12in guns. These were capable of firing a shell, with some accuracy, at targets up to 3 miles away. Ironically, in spite of her heavy artillery, her greatest success in the First World War came when she rammed and sank a German submarine. From the day of her launch in 1906 she made virtually all other warships obsolete: nothing could match her speed and armament, and the race was on to build even faster and deadlier warships. The man who masterminded the building programme was Admiral Sir John Fisher. When he wrote an official report on the ship, he started with a joke: 'New Name for the Dreadnought: "The Hard-Boiled Egg". Why? Because she can't be beaten.'

These great and innovative ships represent the pinnacle of achievement for the British shipbuilding industry. It dominated the world markets, producing a million tons of shipping in 1892 for the first time, and that figure had increased by 70 per cent by the time war broke out in 1914. But already there were worrying signs. Other nations might not have the same production, but they were growing at a far faster rate. In the same period the production from American yards went up by 197 per cent and the Germans by an even more impressive 377 per cent. And there were new nations joining in the fray. Japan had started ordering large numbers of ships from British yards, but as part of the deal the builders had to provide a complete set of working plans and specifications. Shortly after a ship was delivered from Britain, duplicates were on the stocks in Japan.

Much of the story of the development of ships in the nineteenth century has been about British innovation and invention. That too was starting to change. In 1892 the German engineer Rudolf Diesel designed a new type of engine, running on oil. The Danish shipbuilders Burmeister and Wain were the first to use a diesel engine in a ship in 1904: appropriately it was an oil tanker. For the time, at least, it seemed to offer a very small threat to the well-established steam engines that powered all British-built ships. It was, however, a hint that the British could not expect a monopoly on new ideas and inventions, and should have provided a spur to the country's builders to think very carefully about their own research programmes. But, for the time being at least, British shipbuilders and British-built ships were the undoubted monarchs of the maritime world.

Rivets being heated on braziers on the keelson of the steamer Montrose *in the early twentieth century.*

Industrial disputes

Advances in technology were not necessarily accompanied by advances in working methods and industrial relations. In fact, if anything, labour relations were worse than they had been in earlier generations. Harland and Wolff, for example, may have been recognised as one of the leaders of the industry in some ways, but a dispute of 1895 is a classic case of how not to manage such affairs. The 1880s had seen a slump in the trade, but when things began to improve yards around Britain granted pay increases. The Belfast riveters asked for their rates to be matched with those on the Clyde, but the company argued that as they were building ships under contracts based on the old rates they could not afford the increase. The riveters went on strike, and the company responded by closing the yard and throwing everyone out of work, strikers and non-strikers alike. But the company were well aware that things were booming in the industry and there was a demand for skilled labour. They began to worry that the new unemployed would simply abandon Belfast and go to work elsewhere. They hit upon a most unlikely plan to prevent this happening. They asked their colleagues in the employers' associations to lock out a quarter of their workforce. Amazingly this plan was agreed, and thousands of men on the Clyde, who had no quarrel with anyone, suddenly found themselves out of work.

Even commentators who were generally well disposed to the employers saw that if the employers could act like this to support one of their members, then so too could the workers. At first nothing happened, but then the yards of the north-east of England began laying off their workforce to support Belfast and Glasgow. With skilled men outside the gates, essential work was passed out to apprentices. It was the final straw. The inevitable strike was called, and work in all the main yards in Britain was brought to a halt. Eventually Harland and Wolff offered a small rise, which would have been accepted when the dispute began but was now rejected. The company responded by opening the gates to anyone who would break the strike, and offering them protection. Inevitably, as in so many cases, poverty won over principle and there was a slow return to work. The price that had been paid for what should have been a purely local dispute was enormous, with shipbuilding brought to a halt across the whole country.

Disputes between employers and workers were inevitably disruptive, but it was the disputes between one group and another that were to prove at least as damaging to the efficient running of the industry. In the previous chapter we looked at some of the ways in which new men with new skills were introduced into an age-old industry. If the changes had been clear-cut and unambiguous then problems might have been avoided, but the divisions were never really distinct. If you look at some of the work of the shipyard, it becomes clearer: two good examples can be found in the jobs of shipwrights and caulkers.

Shipbuilding begins with designs and the next few stages changed little in essence from the days of wooden sailing ships. The plans were taken to the mould loft, where they were converted into full-size chalk outlines on the floor. These were transferred to the body plan, a series of cross-sections of the hull, each relating to one frame. These were then scrieved, gouged into wooden boards and these were used to create wooden templates. It is only now that differences appear: instead of carving wood to fit the template, iron and steel were bent to shape. The question now was: how much of this work went to a shipwright and how much to an engineer working in metal? And, just as importantly, would they have the same standing in the hierarchy and the same pay?

Caulking was just as essential in an iron hull as it had been in a wooden one, but the methods used for the new material were entirely different from those used for the old. Where two plates abutted, the caulker cut a groove in one of the plates, which forced the metal up into a ridge alongside it. He then hammered the ridge flat to overlap the adjoining plate to make a watertight seal. The men were still caulkers, but the job had nothing to do with stuffing oakum into gaps between planks. The same questions of status and pay had to be answered. Shipyards became workplaces where the naming of a job and its allocation were of vital importance. To an outsider it might look petty and even downright stupid, but it made a huge difference to the life of the individual worker. Shipyards did their best to bring order to this Byzantine system by setting up arbitration panels. Reading their judgements today gives an insight into how complex the problem was and how it hampered the drive towards greater efficiency.

In the 1890s the Tyneside arbitrators were asked to settle the question of who should make the wooden spars for a ship's storeroom, joiners or shipwrights. After long deliberation the work went to the joiners, unless any of the spars was bigger than 1½in thickness, in which case it went to a shipwright. One can only imagine what this meant for the smooth completion of what should have been a simple task, with everything stopping at intervals while a lump of wood was measured, and one workman having to sit back while someone else was called in to fit a couple of pieces that he was not allowed to touch. What astounds the outside observer is the time devoted to seemingly trivial questions. A committee sat specially to decide who should put an 18in square door in a bulkhead. The decision was the seemingly patently obvious one – whoever was building the bulkhead should do the door. Outsiders would probably ask why on earth it mattered who put in the little door, as long as the job was properly done. It mattered to the men because shipwrights and joiners were on different pay scales. Originally the shipwrights had been the most important men in the yard, but their status had slipped and by the end of the nineteenth century the joiners were better paid. Not surprisingly this caused resentment and problems. A dispute on the Tyne in 1893 was all too typical.

The Tyne Shipbuilders, representing the various yards along the river, had tried to impose a 5 per cent cut in pay for the joiners. Their argument was that the yards were losing orders because their prices were higher than other yards in Britain. Similar cuts had been accepted by other unions, but the joiners refused and 606 men from 13 companies went on strike. It was clear that the dispute was as much about the special status of the joiners as skilled craftsmen as anything else. In discussions the employers' association made it very clear that, in fact, much of the work could just as easily be undertaken by other tradesmen. They even suggested establishing a joiners' workshop in Holland to take over much of the work. Unlike many trade disputes it was equally clear that the other trades had no sympathy for the joiners' case: they simply would not accept that their status gave them special rights. In the event the joiners had little choice other than to accept the reduction and go back to work, but it did little to improve the working relationships within the various yards. It was just such disputes that led to the different trades taking unmovable positions and fighting all attempts to impose more flexible working patterns.

Lack of co-operation was not limited to the workforce and many employers were also liable to cling on to outmoded practices. The men who started the great companies often had great vision, and based their empires on their own inventive genius and abilities. Their successors were not always of the same calibre and as companies grew larger they needed to draw on the skills of more than one man at the top. Sir Andrew Noble had been a huge influence at Armstrong's Elswick works, and was there when the company merged with an old rival in weapons' manufacture, Whitworth's to become Armstrong Whitworth. When Armstrong himself retired, Noble took over. He was then 70 years old and the business had hugely expanded and was involved not just in armaments but also in building naval and merchant ships. Noble was something of an autocrat who in his later years had little interest in new ideas, especially if they came from junior directors. When one of these, Henry Whitehead, made a proposal that would have saved £30,000 on the lighting bill, Noble's only response when it was raised at a board meeting was a frosty 'I don't think so'. Junior board members were not supposed to have ideas, and if they did they certainly should not have the temerity to raise them at meetings. Initiative was stifled. Even more worrying was Noble's attitude to the rest of the world. In his eyes the company was the greatest battleship builder in the world and it was up to the world to come to him, not for him to look for orders from them. He seldom left Newcastle and refused to set up a London office. But Armstrong Whitworth no longer had a monopoly.

Vickers, based on the Cumberland coast at Barrow, had established their reputation in the 1880s by manufacturing a new type of warship, the submarine. They took the trouble to make sure their voice was heard in government circles. When they complained to the Foreign Office that not enough was being done to promote British yards to potential foreign customers the government stepped in to offer official support for a bid to manufacture a battleship for Japan. Armstrong had already been offered a verbal agreement that they would get the contract, but the weight of officialdom carried the day for Vickers. Whether this was an example of duplicity on the part of Vickers or complacency on the part of Armstrong Whitworth depended on where you stood in the argument.

The truth was that as Noble's time came to an end there was a good deal of jockeying for position at the works, and the new men were not of the same calibre. The commercial arm of the Armstrong Whitworth company was under the control of a man named Swan. He accepted an old steamer in part payment for a new ship and then, rather less sensibly, accepted a second as well. When asked why, he gave the less than convincing reply that he thought two steamers would be easier to sell than one. In fact, he thought he had a buyer in a deal organised by a Canadian consortium. Swan was to sell them his steamers, but he was also to hand over £35,000 in order to acquire lucrative contracts to build ships for a company called Transports Canadiens. Eventually it transpired that the Canadians were using the connection with Elswick to give themselves a spurious respectability in order to acquire mail-carrying rights, while at the same time convincing the British company that they already had the support of the Canadian government so could be relied on for lucrative orders. Fortunately the device was discovered before any real harm was done, but the incident was symptomatic of a deeper malaise within the company. They were suffering from a problem that can always threaten the future of even the most successful business: complacency. It was just one of many signs that unless the vigour of the pioneering days and the desire for innovation were maintained, then the golden age of British shipbuilding might not last for ever.

Small yards and local archives

The period from the middle of the nineteenth century to the outbreak of the First Word War was one of dramatic changes, which had profound effects on both how and where men worked. Shipbuilding in London virtually came to an end. The Millwall yard that had seen the launch of the *Great Eastern* closed and by the mid-1860s the site was a wasteland. New companies that had been established on the Thames, notably Yarrow and Thornycroft, moved away. Over to the west, Bristol was losing its position as a major port and shipbuilding came to a halt. Only the naval dockyards continued as important employers of shipbuilding in southern England. The big naval yards may have been overwhelmingly important and it is in their pay books that you are most likely to find the name of an ancestor working in shipbuilding in this region. But they did not have a monopoly. Throughout the period there were smaller yards operating in the south, particularly in the south-west. They may not have employed vast workforces, comparable to those of the northern yards, but they were far from insignificant. Appledore in Devon has a long tradition of ship-building, and Appledore Shipbuilders, founded in the 1850s, became famous as a builder of schooners, employing a workforce of hundreds. What is remarkable about this yard is that it has survived right through to the present day. Memories of the older days can be found in the North Devon Maritime Museum in the town. This was one of the more impor-tant yards of the south-west, but others also continued at work throughout this period, though on a far smaller scale. James Goss was typical of many small employers, with modest businesses. He had his yard on the Tamar at Calstock. This was described as little more than a mud bank and a couple of sheds, never employing more than a dozen men making wooden vessels, mainly sailing barges and ketches. Goss himself was illiterate and very much in the old craftsman tradition: his drawing office was his kitchen, where he drew in pencil on a board kept propped up against the wall, ready for use. Mechanisation was non-exis-tent, and he relied on local resources. He chose his own timber from the trees of the riverside Cotehele estate, and cut them to size in a saw pit at the yard.

There is an excellent model of the yard in the museum by the quay at Cotehele, a little further down the river from Calstock. James Goss managed to remain in business into the twentieth century, while making no concessions to the modern world. But the modern world was there, right on his doorstep in the shape of the Tamar paddle steamers that called regularly at Calstock. Among them were the *Princess Royal*, the *Albert* and the *Prince*, all built by Willoughby Brothers, who had their yard just round the coast at Plymouth. They represented the other side of the world of shipbuilding in the region, as unlike Goss as one could imagine. The company had been founded by John Willoughby as an iron foundry in 1844, but by the 1890s they had become important shipbuilders in steel. Willoughby was only one of a number of companies building in Plymouth at this time. Activity in the city was by no means limited to the naval dockyard.

Company and union records

When looking for shipbuilding ancestors in this period it is as well to be aware that there were a large number of these small yards, many of whose

An ornate membership certificate for the Associated Shipwrights' Society.

names have been largely forgotten, but who were very significant in their day. There is a considerable literature dealing with these smaller companies. Their histories have usually been published locally, often by small presses, and they are too numerous to list here. They should, however, be generally available in the local history sections of the larger public libraries. Local archives also hold a good deal of material on companies and by comparing details from census returns with trade directories and other similar sources, it is often possible to narrow the search to two or three likely employers. Although, in some senses, it is more difficult to find information where the yards were small, the industry of minor importance and records scarce, there is also a positive side to the search. Most people worked comparatively close to home, so there are not a huge number of places where a shipwright would have worked. Taking Calstock as an example: names such as those of the Basset family crop up, and one of them, Arthur Basset, can be traced as a former apprentice at the Goss yard.

The growth of the industry and the formation of increasingly powerful owners' associations accelerated the process of union amalgamation. In the iron shipbuilding industry the United Society of Boilermakers and Iron and Steel Shipbuilders incorporated, among others, the Scottish Society of Boilermakers, the first time men working north and south of the border were represented by the same union. Their records from 1872 are held in the Modern Records Archives at the University of Warwick. The Shipconstructors' and Shipwrights' Association was formed in 1908, after several earlier attempts to bring the various local unions under one organisation. The new union actually incorporated nineteen separate local unions, based as far apart as London and Belfast. In their case, the motive for joining together was not so much the need to present a united front to the employers, as an attempt to try and prevent inroads into their traditional practices by the increasingly powerful boilermakers. Many of their records are held in the Working Class Movement Library in Salford. The big unions make research a good deal easier, because in general their papers are more likely to have been preserved. But researching back through the years before the big amalgamations is trickier. You will need to track down all the various local unions, some of which, such as the London and District Society of Drillers, lasted only a short time – in this case from 1889–1908.

Although a large part of the work force was unionised by the end of the nineteenth century, salaried employees were often not members of any union. While it is easy to spot the occupation of somebody listed in the Glasgow area census as, for example, 'riveter', another listed as 'draughtsman' could just as easily have been employed in another branch of engineering by one of the other major employers, such as the North British Locomotive Company. In the absence of personal documents, then only company records will provide the answer.

This was a period of enormous expansion, concentrated on the big companies, each employing thousands. The constructors who specialised in building warships and armaments prospered hugely, with Vickers rapidly moving to the top of the list with a capital of over £5 million in 1912, a huge sum for those days. The three other major performers in this field each were capitalised at over £2 million. In the mercantile field, there were now twenty-seven limited companies, with an average capital at the beginning of the twentieth century of slightly over £400,000 each. Shipbuilding was big business, and if ever there was a time when one would be most likely to find an ancestor working in the industry, this was it. Production was at a peak and, as mechanisation was only advancing quite slowly, the work force was also as high as it would ever be. Everything was to change in 1914, when Europe went to war.

Chapter Six

WAR AND DEPRESSION

*The First World War – Post-war modernisation – Working practices –
Foreign competition – The* Queen Mary *– The Second World War –
Business archives – Preserved ships*

The First World War

At the outbreak of war in 1914 the work of shipyards changed immediately. More ships were needed and there was an equally urgent demand for facilities for repairing naval and merchant ships damaged in conflict. Many leading yards had already been taking on naval orders, but now these had absolute priority. Scott's of Greenock, for example, built everything from battleships to minesweepers, though they were mainly occupied with building destroyers, twelve of them in all. But their main contribution was to make significant improvements in submarine design. These were based on new developments from Italy, the Laurenti design pioneered by Fiat. The submarines were powered by Fiat-Scott oil engines and were given a hull far closer to the lines of a surface craft. Previously submarines had been almost circular in cross section, which made them very difficult to handle when cruising on the surface. The giant battleships had always been considered the pride of the Navy, but now they were destined to prove far less important than the more modest submarines.

In the past naval warfare had consisted of ships going to sea and blazing away at each other in close combat. Things had changed. The British fleet far outnumbered the German, but the German guns had a greater range. The latter's guns fired at a much higher elevation than ever before, which called for a rapid rethink of the way in which ships were protected. Shells no longer came more or less horizontally towards the target, but were fired in a great arc, so that they landed more like bombs from on high. One of the first urgent tasks facing the yards was to reinforce the deck armour on the warships.

It was generally thought that there would be major engagements that would determine who controlled the seas, but the outnumbered Germans had no intention of coming out to face the British fleet. Instead, they tried to tempt the British warships out of harbour to pick them off piecemeal. Vice-Admiral Scheer, the German Commander in Chief, devised a plan to draw the British by threatening the vital shipping lanes of the North Sea with a battle fleet in 1916. The ruse worked and the British under Admiral Sir John Jellicoe set off for the engagement, their progress monitored by German submarines. The result was the indecisive Battle of Jutland, in which fourteen British and eleven German ships were sunk, with great loss of life, but at the end of the encounter the strategic balance was unchanged. It was the only engagement of its kind during the war, the last occasion when great fleets met at sea to try and blow each other out of the water. The most important result was a decision by Germany to change the nature of their offensive. Up to then their submarines had been ordered to capture prizes: now they were given the order to sink enemy shipping. The emphasis was no longer on size and fire-power, but on speed: the main naval conflict would be between submarine and destroyer. The principal victims would be merchant shipping.

Whatever else it may do, war speeds development. Each advance in technology by one side has to be countered by the other, and then that in turn has to be followed by more advances in an endless game of military leapfrog. One of the great changes was the replacement of coal by oil for the ships' boilers. This brought a huge increase in efficiency, greatly reduced the numbers of stokers needed and gave ships the capability to refuel at sea. The original turbines had worked via direct-drive system, but were improved by the introduction of reduction gearing: the turbine running at far higher speed than the propeller shaft. This made for greater efficiency. One result of these changes was that engines could be made lighter: the engine of a battleship built in 1894 weighed 242lb for each horsepower it produced; by the end of the war that figure was down to 110lb. When the biggest ships of the day were producing 85,000 horsepower, that all adds up to a great deal of weight. Not surprisingly, speed increased rapidly, until it was common to have cruisers with a top speed of 33 knots by 1918.

The yard owners were more than willing to do their bit for the war effort, and so were the workers. That was a problem. For very many workers 'doing their bit' meant signing up and the pressure to do so was immense. In the mood of hysterical patriotism that swept the nation, a man not wearing uniform was liable to be branded a coward, however valuable the work he was doing. The situation was not helped by the recruitment policy of the Ministry of Munitions. An official visited Bartram's yard on the Wear at Sunderland in the hope of recruiting rivet heaters, until the management convinced him that without them work would come to a standstill. There was little point in hauling young men off for the Navy if it meant that there would be no ships for them to serve on. The government did, however, come to understand the importance of shipbuilding and other forms of war work. The Munitions Act of 1915 banned strikes and restrictive practices and allowed the government to move men to where they were most needed. Even so, there was a worrying shortfall in the workforce, and it was necessary to recruit more labour. In the absence of men, there was very little choice: the yards began to employ women. They were not just brought in for the traditional female tasks. Now they were taking on engineering jobs, working machine tools and proving themselves perfectly capable of doing work that had always been a male prerogative. The women were delighted. Left at home to live on a soldier's meagre pay, they were more than happy to try something new and earn a wage of their own. An article in the *Engineer* in 1919 described how quickly the women had mastered

Women workers at a machine shop on the Clyde during the First World War.

technical skills, such as setting and grinding their own tools and even setting machines from working drawings, tasks that had been thought to require long apprenticeships. Not everyone was happy.

No area of British shipbuilding had more militant unions than the Clyde, which earned it the nickname 'Red Clyde'. They saw wartime regulations as just an excuse for exploitation. There was a well-known recruitment poster of the day, showing children looking at a clearly embarrassed father and asking the question: 'What did you do in the Great War, daddy?' The Clydeside version replaced the father with an employer and provided an answer: 'I did the workers'. A new organisation was set up, the Clyde Trades Vigilance Committee, to fight 'dilution', bringing new, untrained workers into the industry, and that included all women. The government was having none of it. They took drastic action, arresting the leaders and rigorously enforcing the conditions of the Munitions Act.

During the war years, the industry had met and overcome all the challenges that had been put to it. It had even experienced the war at first hand, when Zeppelins began to attack shipyards and other targets, eventually raiding as high as the Scottish border. It had been a period of rapid technical advances and radically changed working practices. When peace came in 1918, it was, however, to prove to be business as usual. This was particularly hard on women workers, who had come to enjoy their new skills and decent wages. They were simply told to go back home; the jobs would go back to the men returning from the war.

Post-war modernisation

It must have seemed that when peace arrived, life in the shipyards would return to what it had been before in other ways as well, with every possibility of order books being filled as shipping fleets looked to recoup the losses of the war years. Optimism was short-lived. The first area to be hit was the construction of naval vessels; the race for national supremacy had left the Navy with all the vessels they were likely to need in the foreseeable future. The small amount of work dwindled to nothing, following the conference on naval shipping that opened in Washington in 1921. It was agreed that there should be a ten-year ban on the construction of new warships, which it was hoped would be an important step towards establishing world peace. It was nothing but bad news for the private shipyards, where naval contracts had represented a quarter of all their work.

The hope was that international trade would increase at a good, steady rate, just as it had before the war. That never happened, and as the market shrank so the competition for new orders became ever more fierce. British yards during the 1920s had the capacity to provide all the new shipping required throughout the world. Unfortunately for them, they did not have a monopoly, and foreign yards were equally busy fighting for orders, while going through intensive modernisation programmes. The maritime cake had remained the same size, but there were far more looking to cut out a slice.

The result was inevitable. Once the replacements for wartime losses had been made good, even the mightiest companies found themselves struggling. John Brown's was typical of many others. In 1920 there were 9,279 men on the books, but by 1921 that had shrunk to 6,322 and the following year there were just 3,653 left, and those who remained found that their pay had been halved during that 3-year period. If they thought things could not get worse, they were wrong. In 1932, the whole edifice tumbled, and all that was left was a skeleton staff of 422 men, just keeping essential maintenance ticking over.

Harland and Wolff were among Brown's greatest rivals, and their empire had expanded out from their base in Belfast, with subsidiaries in England and Scotland. The man in charge, Viscount Pirrie, had taken advantage of the war years to bring order to a Belfast yard that had been notable for disputes. He had used wartime legislation to clear away many of the old restrictive practices. Those who objected to the changes were considered troublemakers, and all Pirrie had to do was inform the recruitment officers that the men in question were no longer essential workers. Those that remained soon got the message: accept the new conditions at the yard or take your place among the cannon fodder in the trenches. It was not a difficult decision to reach. Pirrie may have been dictatorial but he had his reasons. He knew that old practices stood in the way of modernisation, and he had plans for a new type of merchant ship that would be built using modern prefabrication technology. As soon as the peace agreement was signed he began getting in orders, ending up with twenty-one contracts.

Pirrie believed that the systems he had put in place during the war years could be carried over to peacetime. The men had other ideas. They had worked hard for low wages for the common good, and now they wanted a share of the rewards: a shorter working week of 44 hours and higher pay. Management refused and after the now familiar round of strikes, the inevitable compromise was reached and the men settled for a small rise and a 47-hour week. One other shameful demand was put to the management by the Belfast Protestant Association: all Catholic workers should be sacked. That was agreed without an argument.

Pirrie died in 1924 and what had seemed like a solidly built company with full order books suddenly seemed fragile. The finances were based on loans, and an attempt to bolster the funds with a share issue failed: just one-eighth were actually sold. The order book might have looked healthy, but when the figures were looked at more closely, it was found that the jobs had been so badly costed that the company would not merely fail to make a decent profit, they stood to lose £750,000. In 1927 the company books showed a loss for the year, a big overdraft and unpaid bills. The government was asked to help out and they had little choice. This was Belfast's biggest employer and the possibility of handing the republican movement such a huge propaganda weapon simply could not be contemplated. The Treasury sent in experts to try and sort out the finances and they found things even worse than they feared. Harland and Wolff's liabilities came to a startling £30 million. The final blow came with the Wall Street Crash of 1929, which sent financial institutions around the world into a state of panic. From 1931 to 1934 not a single ship went down the Belfast slipways.

Not everyone suffered to the same extent. As mentioned in the last chapter, Armstrong had lost their way and was feeling under increasing pressure from Vickers. The answer was to amalgamate the two companies under a management that had progressive ideas. They used the time when the work was slack to put in hand a big modernisation programme, which enabled them to compete on the international market. They were severely hampered, however, by government policy. In 1925 the Chancellor, Winston Churchill, announced that Britain was returning to the gold standard, with the exchange rates back at pre-war levels. This it was argued was absolutely essential to restore confidence in the country's financial institutions. Whatever it might have done for the banking system, it was a catastrophe for an industry fighting for orders against keen competition. The immediate effect was to raise the value of the pound by about 10 per cent: which, in practice, raised the price of every estimate given to a foreign customer. The 'strong pound' was a mantra chanted by conventional economic experts. There was one voice loud in disagreement – Maynard Keynes. He prophesied a deep depression and a dark period of social unrest and disputes. Prophets of gloom, from Cassandra onwards, are very rarely as appealing as those who assure everyone that everything will turn out fine. Keynes was another Cassandra who was to prove all too accurate in his predictions.

In 1930 Sir James Lithgow of Fairfield came up with a proposal for keeping the big yards in business. He set up the National Shipbuilders Security, a consortium of successful companies, who would band together to buy up ailing yards with a guarantee that they would be kept closed for at least forty years. There was a cold logic to this industrial version of Darwinism. There was not enough work for everyone, so the weak must be sacrificed so that the fit could survive. One of the closures was Palmer's of Jarrow on the Tyne. It was by far the most important employer in the town, and in desperation the men of Jarrow set out for London to put their case to Parliament. The Jarrow March became famous as a symbol of the great depression. It received huge amounts of public sympathy, but nothing else. Shipbuilding at Jarrow was ended. The miseries of unemployment were, if anything, made worse by the attitude of those in authority who provided relief.

Working practices

Daniel Murray started work as a plater's boy at Greenock in 1928. Like many others he was out of work for a time, but eventually got a job at £2 18s a week. At which point, the authorities stopped his father's dole completely, leaving the teenager as sole wage earner for a family of eight. He had no choice but to leave home, but was then seen going back on a visit, so the family's dole was cut again. His story was recorded as part of an oral-history project carried out by the McLean Museum in Greenock, and it also provides fascinating information on working methods at the time. As a helper in a plating gang he had no security. The platers were members of what was known as the shell squad, putting the outer shell on the ship. They worked on a fixed contract and in bad weather they were quite liable to decide to go home – or more usually round to the pub. They were still being paid: their helpers, who were paid by the gang not by the yard, got nothing. Safety standards on the job were unknown. Today hard hats and industrial boots would be compulsory. Then nothing was provided and most men wore flat caps and whatever footwear they could afford. The riveters generally worked stripped to the waist, simply because of the physical demands of the job. As a member of a plating gang, Murray had to handle sheets of heavy steel and had to manufacture his own industrial gloves out of strips of leather, but even then he frequently suffered from gashes to his hands from the razor-sharp edges. The worst task was screwing up, fastening the heavy plates in position, ready for riveting. This was often done while standing on a cradle of two suspended planks, hung out below the curve of the hull.

Wherever one looks in the story of shipbuilding at this time there is the same sense of an industry that had never quite got used to the idea that it would not automatically retain its position at the top of the international league tables. Some of the reluctance to accept change is very understandable. One of the toughest jobs involved cutting off the protruding heads of countersunk rivets by hand. The oxyacetylene burner should have made the work far easier, but its introduction was resisted by the workforce. In times of high unemployment no one welcomed a device that would reduce

An aerial view of the Clyde in the 1930s, showing ships still being built on open berths.

the number of men needed to do a job. There were major changes during this period. Welding was slowly beginning to take over from riveting, for example. The advantages were obvious. A riveted hull is covered by knobbly rivet heads; a welded hull is smooth – a smooth hull will slip more easily through the water. For the workforce it meant the end of the deafening pounding of the riveter, but it was only replaced by equally damaging noxious fumes.

It was not only the men who shied away from innovation. Companies, too, were reluctant to invest in new plant and equipment. There was an argument that said that when times were hard, capital tied up in machinery was capital wasted, while workers could simply be sacked and re-employed when things improved. Astonishingly, there were companies that preferred to use the old riveting gangs with their heavy hammers, rather than investing in hydraulic riveters. In other industries, production lines were improving efficiency, but in all but the more forward-looking shipyards, things went on as they had done for generations. Their foreign competitors took a very different view.

Foreign competition

While Britain still concentrated on building steamers, continental yards were increasingly turning to motor vessels. Instead of thinking on a one ship at a time basis they planned for the long term. They were able to offer owners payment schedules spread over many years, terms that were particularly attractive in times of hardship. As a result they had full order books and were able to plan a logical flow of materials and work. In many countries, financing development was far easier than it was in Britain. Banks were willing to offer loans and governments were prepared to subsidise the industry. In these circumstances, Britain found it difficult to compete in the overseas market. Paradoxically British yards even suffered as a direct result of the reparations made by Germany after the First World War. The Germans had handed over a number of old merchant ships to British lines. They may not have been the latest thing in marine engineering, but they did the job and filled gaps that might otherwise have been filled by new ships from British yards. It seemed to many British shipbuilders that they were not only fighting overseas competitors, but also struggling against bad decisions made by their own government. Dealing with Whitehall bureaucracy was time consuming and frustrating. Sir A M Stephen of Stephen's of Linthouse hunted for Admiralty orders, but found it difficult to get any business done: 'They don't seem to arrive back from lunch till nearly half past 3'.

The *Queen Mary*

Eventually, the government did begin to offer help. In 1935 they developed a 'scrap and build' programme, which allowed owners who scrapped old ships to get special loans to order replacements from British yards. The sums involved were comparatively small, only amounting to an average of £60,000 per ship, but fifty ships did get built under the scheme. No one was going to build a ship on the scale of the great liners of the past on that sort of money, but Cunard were still desperate to get a new ship for the Atlantic that would take over the starring role once held by the *Mauretania*. Negotiations began in 1930 between Brown's and Cunard. There were extended talks on the specifications. Speed was still considered paramount, and the new ship was required to have a speed in excess of 30 knots. It was a big undertaking for Brown's. They had to invest in new machinery, pay for improvements to the Clyde so that the big ship could be safely launched and negotiate with around seventy sub-contractors. There was one requirement insisted on by Cunard: everything had to be British. Eventually a

Early days in the construction of the Queen Mary *at John Brown's on the Clyde.*

price was fixed: just £8,000 short of £4 million. This was to be not only the fastest but also the most luxurious liner afloat, incorporating such novelties as air-conditioning. Plans were agreed and then the depression hit. Work had hardly started before everything came to a standstill at the end of 1931.

It was only in 1934 that, thanks to a million-pound government loan, work restarted. At the end of the year, she was ready for the launch and needed a name. Up to then she had simply been prosaic Ship No. 534. Now she was to be the *Queen Mary*. She was fitted out with the latest technology, with her four propellers driven by geared turbines. She was not just modern: she looked modern as well. Out went state rooms that looked like Victorian gentlemen's clubs accidentally set afloat. Instead the interior was designed in the fashionable clean, crisp art deco style, and even the third-class passengers were assured of modern entertainment with their own cinema. The ship was, quite simply, a triumph and passengers loved her. She was to have a sister ship, the *Queen Elizabeth*, also built at Brown's, but she was still being fitted out in 1939 when war was declared. Instead of starting her working life taking passengers to New York she was sent off to take troops to battle.

The Second World War

Just as in 1914, the outbreak of war brought all the work the shipyards needed. It also brought government control with the inevitable red tape. Not surprisingly, the shipbuilders resented being told what to do and how to do it by bureaucrats with little or no experience of the industry. One yard even produced their version of a morning prayer to be said in government offices. It began:

> O Lord, grant this day we come to no decisions, neither run into any kind of responsibility, and that all our doings may be ordered to establish new departments from day unto day, and that we do always that which will make us sit tight. Grant, we beseech Thee that our duplicates and triplicates multiply fruitfully so that we, being defended from fear of insecurity, may pass our time (and the taxpayers' money) in rest and quietness.

As during the First World War, women were called in to help out, and they proved themselves capable of performing every kind of job, from plating to crane driving. It is sometimes forgotten that the war brought great pressures to bear on the whole family. With a father away in the forces and the mother working long hours at the yard, children had to become self-reliant at a very early age. In later life, a Tyneside man remembered coming home from school and instead of doing his homework he had to go into the kitchen to get the evening meal ready for when his mother came back from the yard. There was one very big difference between the two wars, however. In the first, the Zeppelin raids caused comparatively small amounts of damage. In the second, the bombers reached shipyards everywhere in Britain. Among those most severely hit was Harland and Wolff in Belfast. The raids began in April 1941 and culminated in the great raid that began on the night of Easter Monday and only ended at 4 am the next day. A total of 180 German bombers took part, and although the shipyard was one of the main targets, little of the city was spared. It was the worst single raid outside of London for its ferocity, which left 900 dead and an estimated 100,000 homeless. It did not stop the yard from working throughout the war. At the height of activity there was a workforce of 35,000 turning out naval ships of all kinds, right up to cruisers and aircraft carriers, as well as building and repairing merchantmen. Similar stories of devastating raids could be told of ship-yards throughout Britain.

There is a tendency to think of war work as being mainly involved in the construction and repair of warships. This was not really the case. There was an immense loss of merchant shipping, as a result of the German U-boats, and this had to be replaced to keep essential supply lines open. The yards turned out over 7 million tons of new merchant vessels and there was an equally large workforce occupied in repairing damaged craft. By the end of 1945, shipbuilding and marine engineering was employing nearly 350,000 workers. It was a frantic time but not, however, a time of innovation. Roughly two-thirds of the cargo ships were still steamers and over three-quarters of those were still fitted with piston engines and not turbines. The majority of hulls were still riveted. It is perhaps understandable that in the desperate circumstances of war it seemed prudent to stay with what was known and trusted, but other countries had different ideas. It was symptomatic of what was to come in the post-war years that not everyone shared the conservative attitude of the British.

In America a huge shipbuilding programme was put in hand, all based on the latest technology. Ships were no longer built as entire hulls from the keel up, but in prefabricated sections, initially quite small, but later rising to 200-ton units. The demands of wartime called for basic merchant ships that could be easily assembled, and the end result was the fleet of Liberty Ships, many of which were sent across the Atlantic to Britain. In all nearly 3,000 of these craft were built, and one of the most important features was the welded hull. Welding was far faster than riveting. In a publicity exercise, the *Robert E. Peasy* was launched less than five days after the keel was laid.

The advantages of welding were obvious. It was not just faster but eliminated one whole step of the production process. There was no need to caulk the joints between plates. The disadvantages were not so clearly understood. There were a number of catastrophic failures, and many regarded the new technique with great suspicion. An American-built escort carrier was known to its British crew as the 'Woolworth carrier', because it was cheaply put together and considered hopelessly unreliable. Some of the faults were due to poor workmanship, but the main problem was an intrinsic one of stress fractures in the plates. The very high temperatures used in welding resulted in localised heating of the adjoining plates, and when that was followed by rapid cooling, it set up stresses in the metal. This could cause an almost invisible network of tiny stress cracks. Similar stresses could occur in riveted hulls, but these could be absorbed because the rivets themselves gave way, easing the problem. The riveted seams had no give in them, and the result could be a major fracture. The most spectacular example occurred just after the war at Boston where the tanker *Ponagansett* was undergoing a minor repair. A small clip was being welded to the deck when the whole ship split wide apart. Those who doubted the wisdom of changing from riveting to welding appeared to be justified, but a detailed investigation of welding by the US National Bureau of Standards correctly identified the causes, and a whole new set of regulations was introduced which effectively solved the problems.

Business archives

The story of the 1920s and 30s makes grim reading, with the numbers employed in the industry in 1932 down to little more than a quarter of what they had been in 1920. It was not just a question of yards cutting their staff, but of yards being closed and disappearing altogether. Many men who were highly skilled and trained for one of the branches of shipbuilding could all too easily spend long periods out of work. There was little prospect of finding employment of a similar nature anywhere else, as the slump hit all sections of engineering. The old tradition of loyalty to an employer, with son following father into a particular yard was broken: anyone would take any job wherever it became available. It makes the task of following a particular career in detail extremely difficult. The only positive aspect of researching this period is that, the nearer one gets to the present day, the better chance there is of finding archive material, in the company and union records discussed in earlier chapters. One valuable source, however, is no longer available: the census returns for this period will not be made public for many years. This is where researchers will have to rely to a much greater extent on family documents and memories than on official archives. In writing a history of shipbuilding one inevitably starts at the earliest useful date, and works towards the present. Family historians move in the opposite direction. Anyone in doubt about how to deal with this period should turn back to Chapter One for some basic information.

Preserved ships

Having stressed the problems, one should not be dispirited: there is a lot of information available. Looking at one aspect of the period, warship construction, a good place to get an idea of the huge advances made in the period from the late nineteenth century to the Second World War is to pay a visit to the Chatham Historic Dockyard, to see two restored ships.

HMS *Gannet* was built at Sheerness in 1878 and is unmistakably Victorian. Constructed out of teak planking on an iron frame, she could be powered by either sail or steam, and carried light guns on her upper deck. She was one of the famous gun boats that patrolled the waterways of Empire. By way of complete contrast one can turn to HMS *Cavalier*, a destroyer built in 1944, not at one of the great yards, but at J Samuel White's on the Isle of Wight. It is a useful reminder that small yards such as this had a vital role to play in the war years, and anyone connected with the yard will find excellent archive material in the maritime museum and library at Cowes. White's is by no means unique, and a number of small yards made important contributions to the war effort. Of course, the big yards turned out a far greater volume of shipping – and vessels on a far grander scale. The cruiser HMS *Belfast*, now to be found near Tower Bridge in London, was, as the name suggests, built in that city at Harland and Wolff in 1938. These historic ships give a good overall impression of just how far construction and design moved forward in the first half of the twentieth century. It is unfortunate that there is not the same opportunity to see similar examples from the merchant marine. If you want to visit the *Queen Mary* for example you will have to take a trip to California.

Big ships are glamorous, but the small can have their own attractions. The 1927 steam tug *Portwey*, now preserved in London docks, is a reminder of the multitude of these vessels that once bustled around the country's docks and harbours. The old Clyde Puffer *VIC32* no longer carries cargo, but instead takes passengers on steam holidays around the Scottish west coast. The first half of the twentieth century was a time of bust and boom, war and peace, but was also an age that produced some great ships.

Chapter Seven

DECLINE AND FALL

Failures in British shipyards – Modernisation – Amalgamation –
The shrinking industry

Failures in British shipyards

The problems that had plagued British shipyards in the pre-war years did not disappear when peace was declared. Some were built into the very fabric of the yards. On a busy river like the Clyde, for example, there was a heavy demand for waterfront sites but a limited supply of space. As a result yards had to be fitted into the land available rather than being planned for a smooth flow of materials and processes. New time and motion studies were introduced and the results often made for depressing reading. One study recorded the time it took for a plate to be taken from the store and set in place in the hull. The best time was 436 minutes, of which 236 were taken up with simply moving the piece of steel from one location to another, and only the remaining 200 minutes involved anyone doing any actual productive work. There were, however, many things that could be done to improve efficiency, such as introducing new tools and different working practices. But here, all too often, the old problems of demarcation reappeared. Elaborate rule books covered all aspects of the old working methods, but what was to be done when entirely new production techniques were introduced? The biggest change of these came with the introduction of prefabrication, in which sections were built under cover, and then assembled on the slipway, ready for launching. Someone had to decide which jobs went to which trades in the new technology.

Stephen's of Linthouse was one of the companies that decided to intro-duce this new technology in 1957. A dispute promptly arose between the boilermakers and shipwrights about who should have the lion's share of the work in the new fabrication sheds. J G Stephen quoted an example of how things had worked in the past. He described what happened when metal bars had to be welded to metal plates. The plater put the bar in position, then stood back and waited for the tack welder to fasten it in place. Then the tack welder sat back and waited for the plater to fetch the next bit and set it up, and so it went on. It was a job that one man could have done perfectly well on his own. But the unions could not agree on which man it should be, and the shipwrights went on strike in June that year. In August the union delegates reached an agreement, but the shipwrights on the workforce rejected it. By September, the rest of the work force was unable to move any of the projects forward because of the backlog of shipwrighting work, and Stephen announced that the yard would have to close. At the very last minute there was an agreement to take the whole issue to the Disputes Committee, and accept its verdict. It decided in October that the original proposals were perfectly fair, and the shipwrights should have accepted them. The Chairman's Report for that year spelled out exactly what the dispute had cost. Without it 700 more men could have been employed and sub-contractors would have been asked to supply £2 million worth of extra material, mostly steel, which would have given more work to other industries. Even more important was the loss of confidence among the yard's customers, who began to wonder if any jobs would ever be finished on schedule. It was a disaster for everyone concerned. This sort of disruption was, sadly, common throughout the industry.

The faults in the industry were by no means limited to one side. British companies still seemed to believe that they were the best in the world, and it was up to customers to fit in with the way they had always done things. Contracts were offered on what was known as 'time and lime': the final bill was made up by adding up all the costs and sticking an appropriate profit on top. There were two glaring objections to this method. The customers had no idea how close the final cost would be to the original estimates, and the builders had no incentive to work towards greater efficiency, since they got their percentage profit anyway. Other yards in other countries were quite happy to offer fixed price contracts, confident they could work within budget, and prepared to accept the drop of profits if they didn't. Not only that but many overseas builders had made huge technological advances, making them more efficient than the British. Japan was a prime example.

The difference began with the training. The new generation of Japanese engineers usually studied marine engineering or naval architecture at university and then went on for further practical training at a working yard. They were encouraged to travel overseas to find out what was new in the world, and when they returned they were given positions of responsibility at an age when they were still full of youthful enthusiasm. Wages for shipyard workers were comparatively low by British standards, but a paternalistic management offered all kinds of fringe benefits, from free medical care to cheap company housing. In the workplace they were offered what to British workers would have been unimaginable luxuries, such as bath facilities on site – they did not have to set off for home covered in the oil and grease of the job. The results were to be seen in a hard-working labour force and few serious disputes. The equally important outcome in terms of management was a progressive outlook, a willingness to embrace the new, which resulted in bigger and bigger ships being built, powered by the most up-to-date machinery, mainly diesel engines and gas turbines. Above all, Japanese ships were reliable, thanks to their meticulous checking system, which included using X-ray examinations to show up any weak welds. As if that were not enough, the Japanese offered to spread the cost of the ship, by offering 70 per cent of the total cost as a loan repayable over seven years at a modest interest rate. The British could only offer to finance 50 per cent and at a higher rate. There was one other key factor, which was not perhaps so immediately obvious, but made a big difference to the essential client-builder relationship. The British had traditionally regarded owners as people who, once they had signed a contract, should simply leave the job in the hands of the experts and go away until they were told the work was finished. The Japanese, and the new generation of European builders, treated the clients as partners, who were to be an important part of the whole production process.

Modernisation

Not all the problems in British yards were of their own making. Britain ended the war in a desperate economic position, and the yards faced shortages of basic materials, especially steel, while inflation made it all but impossible to work out final costings. These difficulties might have been overcome if the issues had been squarely faced. They were not. While productivity was rising, wages were rising even more rapidly. The Wear Shipbuilders Association worked out a productivity index, measured on the simple formula of dividing the gross tonnage of ships produced by the number of men employed. Between 1950 and 1959, productivity rose by nearly 40 per cent, while at the same time wages rose by over 80 per cent. Everyone knew that the answer lay in modernisation, but that cost money that only the biggest yards could afford to spend. Fairfield, for example, built a fine new fabrication shed, served by powerful overhead cranes, which helped them build far bigger ships than ever before. It was much admired, but cost the company £3 million.

Other companies put in hand equally impressive modernisation programmes. Cammell Laird constructed a new dock, served by what was then Britain's biggest crane, a 100-ton monster that rose above the Mersey to the height of the famous Liver Building on the opposite bank. More importantly they brought in new technology. The old system of drawing parts, then making wooden templates from them and using those as guides for cutting the steel was abandoned. In its place they brought in the Monopol system, which reduced drawings to 1:100 scale and these were used to guide automated cutters. It was the beginning of a process that would eventually lead to computerised cutting systems. This was forward looking, but in general the money spent on research and development in British yards averaged at no more than 1 per cent of turnover, a fraction of the money allocated by overseas competitors. It is sad but true that almost without exception in the key areas of management, industrial relations and modernisation, Britain was not keeping pace with other countries. This was enough, in itself, to create a crisis in the industry, but other factors made the situation even worse.

The high prestige ships of the pre-war years were the ocean liners. In the 1950s the first jet-powered airliners appeared on the scene. Suddenly the time taken for an Atlantic crossing was reduced from days to hours. The result was inevitable: by the end of the 1960s there were forty times as many passengers crossing the Atlantic by air as there were by sea. Even so, Cunard decided they needed a replacement for their older flagships, and in 1964, work started at John Brown's on what was to become the *Queen Elizabeth II*, but she was designed from the first to have a dual role, as both conventional passenger liner and cruise ship. She was to be the last in a long line of transatlantic liners.

The 1960s saw the arrival of a new type of ship – the super-tanker. An important landmark was passed in 1962 when the very first tanker to take a load of over 100,000 tonnes of crude oil left Kuwait. It was the start of a movement to even bigger vessels, the very large crude carriers (VLCCs), which most of the British yards, sited along rivers, were not able to build, even if they used the most advanced technology. There was quite simply not enough space to launch them. In the past the yards could always rely on their customers in the British shipping companies, but these too were disappearing. More and more ships were registered overseas, taking 'flags of convenience' and the really big orders were being placed by comparative newcomers, such as the rapidly expanding Greek fleet. None of these owed allegiance to anyone other than the yards offering cheap prices and reliable delivery dates. Neither of these could be guaranteed in Britain. The official government report on the industry produced in 1962 under the chairmanship of J M Geddes highlighted the position. At that time there were sixty-two shipyards in Britain, but only twenty-seven of them were able to build anything bigger than 5,000 tons. It rehearsed the various problems described above and then set out what needed to be done.

Most of the recommendations were obvious. Design needed to be improved and had to make use of the newly developing computer technology. New marketing techniques had to be deployed, not just to sell the end product but to establish what the customers wanted at the time and were likely to want in the future. Whatever companies might think about research and development – and many still regarded it as a waste of time – they must learn to accept that their customers would expect it, and if there was no evidence of an active programme at a yard they would look elsewhere. It also became clear that if the government wanted to save British shipbuilding they were going to have to intervene.

Harland and Wolff benefited from government grants and a new management team, as a result of which they were able to get an order for Britain's first VLCC. But the finances were still rocky and the company found it necessary to go cap in hand to Westminster to ask for a £13.5 million hand out. They got £5.5 million, but that was at least enough to give them the chance to compete for more VLCC orders for Esso and to enter the new, lucrative market for deep-sea oil rigs. Even so the company remained mired in debt and was soon looking for new loans and grants. With sectarian violence becoming ever more serious, no British government was going to let Belfast's biggest employer close its gates.

Another yard that tried to find a new route towards modernisation was Fairfield's. In October 1965, with no previous warning, the management announced the yard was closed. There was an immediate protest, and the cause was taken up in Parliament by the local MP for Govan, John Robin. He managed to get government support and persuaded an industrialist who was known to favour setting up new forms of co-operation between workers and management to take over. Iain Stewart tried to keep clear of politics, and argued that he must have got the balance about right, since he was known to the Labour Party as 'that bloody Tory' and to the Tories as 'that bloody Communist'. His first task was to try and end the old system of restrictive practices, so that a new age could begin where jobs were divided up as needed and not according to the archaic divisions of the official rule book. The shop stewards were livid, but the national union spelled out exactly what was at stake: either accept the new proposals or join the dole-office queue.

One advantage of having a new man from outside the industry was that he asked questions that never occurred to those who had been part of it all their lives. Why, for example, did work on a ship always start at the bows? To which the answer was that it had always been like that. But in the new ships, such as the VLCCs, all the machinery and living quarters were in the stern. If you started there, then fitting out could carry on while the rest, which was largely storage tanks, was built. There were other more subtle differences. Anyone walking into a shipyard could tell the foremen from the rest by their bowler hats. Fairfield introduced hard hats, which were more practical, but which gave an indication that everyone was working towards the same ends. Even more startling was the regular presence of senior management on site. Old divisions were disappearing and it was made clear that men who worked hard and showed initiative could expect promotion, right up to board level. Proper training schemes were introduced and even the time and motion men, with their clipboards and stopwatches, were accepted. Some ludicrous practices were revealed. An excellent example comes from another yard, where there were regular stoppages for stocktaking which seemed to take an unreasonably long time. One man was found laboriously counting all the washers in the store. They were all standard sizes, and it had never occurred to anyone to find out what a single washer weighed and then simply weigh the whole load to find out how many there were. By eliminating wasteful practices and streamlining work, Stewart was able to turn a thumping loss to a modest profit in just two years.

Amalgamation

Fairfield's appeared to be a success, but the Geddes report had created a new orthodoxy. The main conclusion was that the future lay with big

The modern dockyard at Devonport, with the original covered slip on the right and modern facilities to the left.

yards, employing at least 8,000 and able to turn out a minimum of 400,000 gross tons a year. That would have to happen through amalgamations. Fairfield's was too small to fit into the proposed reorganisation.

Tony Benn, the Minister of Technology, was providing an incentive for mergers on the Clyde and Tyne, with £2,000 million credit for ship owners who placed orders and £20 million to help with the process of amalgamation. A new body was set up, the Ship Building Industry Board, with an unlikely trio at the top, one from the motor-car industry, one from ladies' hosiery and the leader of the miners' union. They pressed the Clyde yards hard and eventually a consortium, Upper Clyde Shipbuilders (UCS), was set up based on five yards: John Brown, Charles Connell, Fairfield, Alexander Stephen and Yarrow. Some were more willing to join than others. Anthony Hopper was the man in charge and he expected to follow the new pattern of management-union co-operation that had proved a success at Fairfield's. He was soon to find out just how difficult that would be. He arrived at the second joint meeting and it began with the usual formalities of approving the minutes of the last meeting. It went to the vote, and all the management indicated approval and the trade unionists sat doing and saying nothing. Exasperated Hopper tried again with the same result. The management side provided an explanation. In Hopper's own words: 'A voice at my side said "those buggers don't get a copy of the minutes, just us".' It was not an encouraging start.

UCS was to prove an expensive failure, in spite of receiving more and more subsidies. Many of the problems were simply old difficulties revisited, but there was also a new difficulty. Because of the high level of government subsidies, changes in government could result in complete changes in policy. Sir Keith Joseph, the former Conservative minister, looking back on those years, made very clear his own attitude and that of many of his colleagues. Governments, he declared 'are busy infecting nominally privately-owned enterprises with the same sickness, which is basically caused by absolution from having to pay their way'. In the same report on UCS, Professor A J M Sykes was equally damning of both political parties. To make UCS succeed required a concerted and massive effort, but what happened was that money was dribbled in a bit at a time, with no reference to any overall plan. He likened it to the compulsive gambler, who after every loss, puts a bit more money on the next race, convinced it will provide the winner to make everything right again. His final judgment, which applied to both parties, could not have been more damning. 'Never, at any point in the exercise, was Government in command of the situation – its intervention proved to be aimless, feckless and ultimately futile.' In 1971 all funding was withdrawn. There was a famous 'work-in', where the men continued to turn up every day, even

*Bad news:
dockyard workers
at Swan Hunter
hear about
redundancies in
1993.*

though the liquidators had been appointed. In the event, nothing could save UCS. It was the last major attempt to rescue the industry from terminal decline.

The shrinking industry

One by one the great yards have closed. In 2007 I walked along the bank of the Tyne, starting at Wallsend, still dominated by the tall cranes of Swan Hunter. Now they have gone. Further upstream there are even fewer reminders of the once-great Armstrong works. The story can be repeated all around the coast. The yards have gone on Tees and Wear in the north east. Cammell Laird is only a memory on the Mersey and activity has long since come to a halt on the Thames. Even the famous naval dockyards are not immune from change. The work of providing engineering support for the Royal Navy at Devonport is now in the hands of Babcock Marine. Work at Portsmouth has also been contracted to private companies. In 2007 BVT, a company formed by the amalgamation of BAE Systems and VT, formerly the warship builders Vosper Thornycroft, began work on the construction of a destroyer, HMS *Clyde*. It was the first warship to be built at the yard since the 1960s. It might not signify a return to the glory days of old, but it does at least represent real work. In 2008 far bigger projects were agreed for two new aircraft carriers, the *Prince of Wales* and *Queen Elizabeth*. One of the contracts went to Govan, and without it then it is doubtful if shipbuilding on the Clyde could have survived.

Today shipbuilding has suffered the fate of a good deal of British manufacturing industry. What survives is only a small fraction of what existed a century ago. There is no one single factor responsible for the decline and it is not even possible to say which elements were the most important – failure to modernise, poor management, intransigent unions, lack of financial support or simply the fact that yards established in the nineteenth century were not able to rise to the demands of the twentieth and twenty-first centuries. The workforce has diminished from hundreds of thousands to thousands, and it is doubtful if the industry will ever rise again. But those of us who had ancestors working in the industry can look back over a splendid history stretching back for centuries. We might not be able to look at some noble ship and say with pride 'I helped to build that' but we can at least say with just as much pride, 'that is what my family did. They built ships.' And I hope readers will get as much pleasure and satisfaction in making that connection for their own families as the author has had from finding his own roots in an industry that was once the finest in the world.

FURTHER READING

Family history

Apart from those already mentioned in the text, the following can be recommended for readers who are beginners or comparatively new to the subject.

Ellis, M. *Using Manorial Records*, 1997: a concise, practical guide to the manorial system and how to work with the records, published by the PRO

Herber, Mark. *Ancestral Trails*, 2005: a basic guide produced in association with the Society of Genealogists

Swinfield, Geoff. *Smart Family History*, 2006: an intermediate guide, published by the National Archives

Shipbuilding literature

The literature on ships and the sea is immense, although those devoted purely to shipbuilding are far scarcer. The following books will provide valuable background information and introductions to the subject.

Adams, John. *History of Ocean-Going Passenger Steamships 1830–1970*, 1999

Beeler, John. *Birth of the Battleship*, 2004

Burton, Anthony. *The Rise and Fall of British Shipbuilding*, 1994: a general history of the subject from the medieval period to the present day

Burton, Anthony. *The Daily Telegraph Guide to Britain's Maritime Past*, 2003: an illustrated guide to over 300 maritime museums and preserved vessels

Dear, I C B and Peter Kemp (eds). *The Oxford Companion to Ships and the Sea*, 2nd edn, 2005: an invaluable reference book with over 2,600 entries on all aspects of the subject

Griffiths, Denis, Andrew Lambert and Fred M Walker. *Brunel's Ships*, 2000

Lavery, Brian. *Ship*, 2004: a readable and authoritative single-volume history of 5,000 years of maritime history

MacDougall, Philip. *Royal Dockyards*, 1982

Rees's Naval Architecture (1819–20), 1970: a reprint of the work that formed part of Abraham Rees's *Cyclopaedia*, published between 1802 and 1820. It is a complete technical treatise on shipbuilding in Britain at the time of the Napoleonic Wars

Ritchie, L A (ed.). *The Shipbuilding Industry*, 1992: this was mentioned in the text, but it is worth stressing that it is the indispensable guide to the historical records of the industry

Shipyard histories

The following are the available histories of individual shipyards, arranged alphabetically by the name of the yard.

Armstrong
Cochrane, Alfred. *The Early History of Elswick*, 1909
Warren, Kenneth. *Armstrongs of Elswick*, 1989

Barclay Curle
Anon. *The Development of Shipbuilding on the Upper Reaches of the Clyde: Messrs. Barclay Curle & Co. Ltd.*, 1911
Anon. *Launching Ways*, 1953
Anon. *Ships and Shipbuilding, Barclay Curle & Co. Ltd 1818–1932*, 1932

Bartram & Sons
Anon. *Bartram & Sons, Centenary Souvenir of the Company's History*, 1938

Beardmore
Hume, John R and Michael S Moss. *Beardmore, The History of a Scottish Industrial Giant*, 1979

Brocklebanks
Gibson, J F *Brocklebanks, 1770–1950*, 1953

John Brown
Grant, A. *Steel and Ships: the History of John Brown's*, 1950
Johnston, Ian. *Ships For a Nation: The History of John Brown & Co. Ltd.*, 2008

Cammell Laird
Anon. *Builders of Great Ships*, 1959

James P Corry
Caughey, J. *Seize Then the Hour, A History of James P. Corry & Co. Ltd and of the Corry Family, 1123–1974*, 1979

William Denny
Anon. *Denny, Dumbarton, 1844–1950*, 1950
Bruce, Alexander Balmain. *The Life of William Denny, Shipbuilder, Dumbarton*, 1888

Dickenson
Anon. *Dickenson & Co. Ltd., One Hundred Years of Progress*, 1947

William Doxford
Anon. *William Doxford & Company*, 1921

Richard Dunston
Anon. *Richard Dunston Ltd.*, 1953

Earle's of Hull
Credland, A G. *Earle's of Hull, 1853–1932*, 1982

Fairfield
Alexander, Kenneth J W and Carson L Jenkins. *Fairfields: A Study of Industrial Change*, 1970
Anon. *The Fairfield Shipbuilding and Engineering Works*, 1909
Anon. *Fairfield, 1860–1960*, 1960
Paulden, Sydney M and Bill Hawkins. *Whatever Happened at Fairfield's?* 1969

James Goss
Paige, R T. *The Tamar Valley at Work, James Goss*, 1978

Gourlays of Dundee
Lythe, S G E. *Gourlays of Dundee, The Rise and Fall of a Scottish Shipbuilding Firm*, 1964

Grangemouth Dockyard Co. Ltd
Anon. *The Grangemouth Dockyard Company Limited*, 1951

Grayson
Brooks, C. *Grayson's of Liverpool, A History of Grayson, Rollo and Clover Docks Ltd.*, 1956

Harland and Wolff
Moss, Michael and John R Hume. *Shipbuilders to the World: 125 Years of Harland and Wolff*, 1986
Peirson, J G. *Great Ship-builders: The Rise of Harland and Wolff*, 1935

R and W Hawthorn
Browne, B C. *The History of the New*, 1914
Clarke, J F. *Power on Land and Sea: A History of R. & W. Hawthorn Leslie and Co. Ltd.*, 1979

Howden Engineering
Anon. *A Hundred Years of Howden Engineering, 1854–1954*, 1954

Inglis
Inglis, John G. *Inglis, Glasgow*, 1977

Kincaids
Anon. *Kincaids, 1868–1968*, 1968

Lithgow
Reid, J M. *James Lithgow, Master of Work*, 1964

Maccallum
Hume, John R and Michael S Moss, *A Bed of Nails, The History of P. MacCallum and Sons Ltd of Greenock, 1781–1981*, 1981

Napier
Halliday, J M. *Robert Napier*, 1980
Napier, David Dehane. *David Napier, Engineer 1790–1869*, 1912
Napier, James. *Life of Robert Napier*, 1904

Orchard
Crighton, John. *The Famous Orchard Dockyard Past and Present*, n.d.

Palmers

Anon. *Six Years Hard Labour, Palmers Hebburn Co. Ltd 1939–1945*, 1946

Davidson, John R. *From Collier to Battleships: Palmers of Jarrow, 1852–1933*, 1946

Dillon, Malcolm. *Some Account of the Works of Palmers Shipbuilding & Iron Co. Ltd*, 1900

Rea, Vincent. *Palmers Yard and the Town of Jarrow*, 1975

Philip

Anon. *Philip & Son Ltd., A Century of Progress 1858–1958*, 1958

Readhead

Anon. *John Readhead & Sons, A Hundred Years of Shipbuilding at South Shields*, 1965

Richards

Goodey, Charles. *The First One Hundred Years, The Story of Richards Shipbuilders*, 1976

Rowhedge

Anon. *The Launching Years, 1904–1954*, 1954

Thomas Royden

Royden, Ernest. *Thomas Royden & Sons Shipbuilders, Liverpool, 1818–1893*, 1953

Scott's

Anon. *Two Hundred and Fifty Years of Shipbuilding by the Scotts at Greenock*, 1961

Short Brothers

Anon. *Mowbray Quay to Pallion Yard, 1850–1950*, 1950

William Simons

Anon. *A Century of Shipbuilding 1810–1910*, 1910

Smiths
Macdonald, Ian and Len Tabner. *Smiths Dock – Shipbuilders*, 1987

Alexander Stephen
Anon. *A Shipbuilding History 1750–1932*, 1932
Carvel, John L. *Stephen of Linthouse. A Record of Two Hundred Years of Shipbuilding 1750–1950*, 1951
Stephen, Murray. *A Shipbuilding History: Alexander Stephen & Sons 1750–1931*, 1932

Swan Hunter
Anon. *Swan Hunter and Wigham Richardson, Engineers and Shipbuilders*, 1906
Kruger, R. *Launching Ways*, 1953
Rutherford, Wilfred. *The Man who built the Mauretania, The Life Story of Sir George B. Hunter*, 1934

James and George Thomson
Anon. *Half a Century of Shipbuilding Mercantile and Naval with a Description of the Clydebank Works of James and George Thomson*, 1896

Thornycroft
Anon. *Half a Century of Thornycroft Progress*, 1919
Barnaby, K C. *One Hundred Years of Specialised Shipbuilding and Engineering*, 1964

Turnbull, Scott
Long, Anne and Russell. *A Shipping Venture: Turnbull Scott & Company 1872–1972*, 1974

Upper Clyde Shipbuilders
Buchan, Alastair. *The Right to Work – The Story of the Upper Clyde Confrontation*, 1972

Vickers
Scott, J D. *Vickers A History*, 1962
Trebilcock, C. *The Vickers Brothers: Armaments and Enterprise 1854–1914*, 1977

Wallsend Slipway and Engineering
Boyd, William. *The Story of the Wallsend Slipway & Engineering Co. Ltd 1871–1897*, 1911

Whites of Cowes
Anon. *Shipbuilding – From Smack to Frigate From Cutter to Destroyer*, 1928
Anon. *Whites of Cowes Shipbuilders*, 1950

Workman Clark
Anon. *Shipbuilding at Belfast, 1880–1933*, 1935

Yarrow
Anon. *Yarrow & Co. Ltd. 1865–1977*, 1977
Borthwick, Alastair. *Yarrow & Co. Ltd: The First One Hundred Years, 1865–1965*, 1965
Yarrow, Lady Eleanor and E C Barnes. *Alfred Yarrow: His Life and Work*, 1923

INDEX

Numbers in italic refer to illustrations.